Upon Open Sky

www.stickingplacebooks.com

© Guillermo Arriaga 2025
© Sticking Place Books 2025

ISBN 978-1-942782-68-1

Upon Open Sky

Guillermo Arriaga

Sticking Place Books
New York

Many people ask me about my source of inspiration. They imagine it comes from literature or cinema, but for me, it has been life itself. I have been fortunate—if serious mishaps can be called fortune—to experience extremes that have led me to question the fine line between life and death, violence and love, brutality and tenderness.

One of the most significant experiences was a car accident I suffered at the age of 27. I was asleep when the driver lost control, and we plunged into a deep ravine. I awoke to the metallic crunch of the van's roof shattering against rocks—a sound I will never forget. As we tumbled, I caught fleeting glimpses of the dense vegetation, the stones tearing through the metal. After several rolls, we stopped. Only the sound of steam escaping the radiator remained. Beyond that, silence.

Three children were in the back seat. I pulled them out as best I could. Flames were emerging from the engine, and we feared it might explode. I was the only one injured—a shattered nose, facial fractures. I underwent surgery and, within weeks, recovered.

I didn't want to waste that experience. Nine years later, I wrote *Upon Open Sky*, my first script, in which I recounted an accident that takes the life of a father and its repercussions on his children, who fantasize about hate and revenge. For various reasons, the script was never filmed.

It was a stroke of fortune that my children found the original manuscript and, three decades later, decided to co-direct it. The work of Mariana and Santiago highlighted the profound essence of the story: two siblings searching for their father in the spaces that defined his life—the road, the desert, roadside diners, the light, the motels.

The film became a circular act with unexpected branches, life returning to life.

Guillermo Arriaga
Mexico City
December 2024

Upon Open Sky is a story deeply rooted in our family. With its recent premiere, many have wondered if our father wrote this story with the idea that we would someday direct it. The answer is no. This script was written nearly thirty years ago, even before the computer age. The manuscript was kept stored away in boxes, as if waiting for the right moment to be found by us and complete its cycle.

In the late 1980s, Guillermo suffered a car accident that profoundly impacted his life and began to echo in his work. In 1994, when we were children, he wrote this story driven by the fear of not being there to watch us grow up. That accident forced him to question how quickly life can change, and fatherhood brought him face-to-face with unknown fears.

From a young age, both our mother and father insisted that before knowing the world, we needed to know Mexico. We were born in a country diverse in nature, culture, people, and gastronomy—a country with many realities. As part of that discovery, the northern border, particularly Coahuila, became a region we explored repeatedly. We traveled its highways, roadside diners, motels and rural villages, connecting with its people and learning to understand its landscape.

During those trips, our father would tell us the story of *Upon Open Sky*. We were too young to read it, but we knew it by heart. More than eight years ago, we came across the original manuscript. When we read it, we knew it was the first project we wanted to direct. After discussing it, we agreed that this story needed a younger vision to bring it to life. Although our father had always wanted to direct it himself, he acknowledged that the person he was when he wrote it had changed over time.

Since then, our journeys to Coahuila took on new meaning. We couldn't travel through those places without thinking of Salvador, Fernando and Paula, the characters in the story. Every highway, every corner, became a potential location. That's how we began to conceive the film.

In 2022, we finally brought the story to the screen. Filming in the desert was a physical and emotional challenge: extreme temperatures, long distances and unexpected hurdles pushed us to our limits but also deepened our connection with the spaces that mean so much to us. As filming progressed, we realized this story not only closed the cycle of a father worried about his children's future but also allowed us to reconcile with that fear and transform it into something tangible.

What you are about to read represents more than a cinematic project. It is the result of a family bond strengthened through storytelling. A vital part of this project has been Maru, our mother and Guillermo's wife, who has been a witness and an inspiration from his earliest stories, and has always been the foundation of this tribe.

This script brought us together not only as filmmakers but also as a family. *Upon Open Sky* is our way of paying homage to our legacy and sharing with the world what unites us: the passion for telling stories.

Santiago Arriaga and Mariana Arriaga
Directors of *Upon Open Sky*

EXT. COAHUILA HIGHWAY – DUSK

A 1993 Chevrolet Blazer makes its way down the highway through the vast Coahuila Desert.

Super: "Coahuila Desert, 1993."

The four o'clock sun casts long shadows off the sparse trees and endless stretch of white sand.

INT. BLAZER – DAY

FERNANDO VILLA (40) is at the wheel. His son SALVADOR (13) is asleep on the passenger seat next to him.

EXT. GAS STATION/HIGHWAY – DAY

The Blazer continues its solitary path down the highway before pulling off at a gas station. The attendant comes over and Fernando Villa gets out of the car.

>   ATTENDANT
> How much?

>   FERNANDO
> Fill her up.

Stretching as the attendant fills the tank, he peeks in to see his son asleep.

>   FERNANDO
> How far from here to Piedras Negras?

>   ATTENDANT
> About two hours.

The attendant finishes up.

                    ATTENDANT
          That'll be eighty, boss.

Fernando pulls out his wallet and pays. He gets in the Blazer and takes off.

INT. CAR – DAY

They make their way down the highway. Salvador wakes up and rubs his eyes. His dad tousles his hair.

                    FERNANDO
          You got a loose screw in there?

Salvador smiles and shakes his head.

                    FERNANDO
          You hungry?

                    SALVADOR
          A little.

EXT. HIGHWAY/ROADSIDE RESTAURANT – DAY

Salvador and his father enter the restaurant and sit at a table. The place is pretty simple. A poorly mounted deer head hangs on one of the walls. A young woman approaches.

                    WOMAN
          Afternoon.

                    FERNANDO
          Afternoon.

                    WOMAN
          We got grilled meat, pork chops,
          enchiladas, machaca, beans and eggs.

FERNANDO
Bring me three eggs, sunny side up, and beans.

SALVADOR
And some grilled meat and enchiladas for me.

Fernando smiles and reaches out to poke him in the ribs.

FERNANDO
You gonna finish all that?

SALVADOR
I sure am!

FERNANDO
You better.

The boy gets up and heads to the bathroom. He goes in and looks around. The bathroom is shabby, lit by a single hanging bulb.

Salvador tiptoes in, trying to avoid the wet spots on the floor, and pees. He comes back to the table. His dad points down at the plate.

FERNANDO
Dig in before it gets cold.

EXT. HIGHWAY – DUSK

The car pulls away from the restaurant and makes its way down the highway.

INT. CHEVROLET BLAZER – DUSK

> FERNANDO
> Pass me a soda.

The boy takes off his seatbelt, turns around and searches for the cooler in the back seat. There are a bunch of things back there and he doesn't find it.

> FERNANDO
> Can't find the cooler?

> SALVADOR
> Nope.

Fernando turns and points with his hand.

> FERNANDO
> Look under those jackets.

EXT. HIGHWAY – DUSK

The blazer continues driving along the highway. The sun is going down.

INT. CHEVROLET BLAZER – DUSK

Finally, Salvador spots the cooler. He's stretching out to reach it when his father curses.

> FERNANDO
> What the fuck!

The boy turns back around. A trailer is coming head on at them. Fernando slams on the breaks and we hear the sound of burning rubber. He stretches out his arm to hold back his son, who looks terrified.

FADE TO BLACK

On black, we hear the sounds of vehicles colliding and then only the hiss of steam coming from the radiator.

EXT. JUNKYARD – MORNING

Super: Mexico City, 1995

FERNANDO JR. (18) is walking through a junkyard, wearing jeans and a t-shirt, but looking a little too clean–cut for this location. His hair is long and he has a serious look about him. Another young man about the same age, EL CHARRO, is walking with him, wearing the kind of grease–smeared, ragged garments you would expect of a junkyard worker.

Fernando approaches a few smashed-up cars and looks them over. His eyes fall on a car that has been totaled and peeks into a broken window. He turns toward El Charro.

> FERNANDO
> At least two died in here.

El Charro, looking a bit surprised, shrugs.

> FERNANDO
> Don't believe me, Charro? Take a look
> for yourself! There are bloodstains on the
> dash and both seats.

El Charro looks in and shakes his head without saying a word.

> FERNANDO
> Don't believe me, do you? Asshole.

Fernando looks around for another of the junkyard employees and spots him at the edge of the lot, straightening out a pipe. This is COYOTE, who is slim with a thick mustache (about 35). He calls out to him.

FERNANDO
Coyote!

Coyote looks up and gestures as if to say, what's up?

FERNANDO
How many people died in this car?

COYOTE
(*straightening up*)
Which one?

FERNANDO
This blue VW Golf.

COYOTE
The Volkswagen? I think it was three: one man, two women. Their car flipped over on the highway to Acapulco.

FERNANDO
(*turning to El Charro*)
What do you say? Was I right?

EL CHARRO
I don't know why you're doing this, man.

FERNANDO
Because you don't get it.

EL CHARRO
Get what? That you come out here because you got a sick fascination with this?

FERNANDO
When are they bringing in more cars?

> COYOTE
> (*thinking*)
> Thursday or Friday…

> FERNANDO
> I'll be here Friday.

> COYOTE
> All right. See you then.

Fernando leaves the junkyard.

EXT. STREET – NIGHT

Fernando walks in silence down a street in a residential area. He stops in front of a large, colonial-style house. Taking out keys, he opens the door.

INT. HOUSE – NIGHT

Fernando goes into the kitchen. A servant is stirring something on the stove.

> FERNANDO
> Any calls for me, Mercedes?

The servant turns and is about to answer when Fernando's mother enters and interrupts.

> MOTHER
> Nope. No one wants you anymore.

The mother gives him a kiss. The servant turns back to the stove. Fernando opens the fridge. Claudio (50), a tall and friendly man dressed in sports attire, comes into the kitchen.

> CLAUDIO
> What's up, Fer?

Fernando turns to look at him, raises his eyebrows, but doesn't answer. He looks back into the fridge.

> CLAUDIO
> (*to Mother*)
>
> Ready?

> MOTHER
>
> Yup.

> FERNANDO
>
> Where you going?

> MOTHER
>
> To the movies.

> FERNANDO
> (*closing the fridge,
> a jug of milk in his hands*)
>
> Again?

> MOTHER
>
> That's right, son, again.

The mother gives Fernando a kiss on the cheek.

> MOTHER
>
> See you. Be good.

> CLAUDIO
>
> See ya, Fer.

Fernando looks annoyed.

INT. TV ROOM – NIGHT

The TV room is large and comfy. There is a giant screen in the middle of the room, with a sofa and a loveseat. PAULA (18), a thin young woman with a sweet face, is watching television with EDUARDO (22), who is clean-cut and dressed on the formal side. Fernando comes in and barely gives them a glance.

>   FERNANDO
> The match starts in ten minutes.

Paula looks over at him and then turns back to the television.

>   PAULA
> We're watching a movie.

>   FERNANDO
> I told you yesterday I wanted the TV.

>   PAULA
> Don't be an ass. Can't you watch on the
> other one?

>   FERNANDO
> The other one doesn't have cable and I
> don't want to watch the replay.

Paula and her boyfriend just ignore him and continue watching. Fernando, annoyed, stands in front of the television. Paula looks annoyed.

>   EDUARDO
>   (*bothered*)
> Move, would you?

>   FERNANDO
> I asked for the TV.

>   PAULA
> Come on, Fer, let us watch.

>   FERNANDO
> Don't call me "Fer."

EDUARDO
Relax, kid.

FERNANDO
Or what?

Salvador (now 15) enters the room. He notices there is tension.

FERNANDO
Whose turn is it to watch TV?

Salvador, looking perplexed, shrugs.

FERNANDO
You heard me tell Mom I wanted to
watch the match, right?

PAULA
Just let us finish watching the movie.

FERNANDO
Damn it! No one said anything yesterday.

PAULA
Don't beat yourself up about it, Fer.

FERNANDO
Assholes. Don't talk to me like that.

Eduardo stands up, defiant.

EDUARDO
Ohhhh, aren't you the big guy!

Paula yanks on her boyfriend's arm and pulls him back down.

                        PAULA
          Eduardo, sit down.
               (*still talking to Fernando*)
          It's just half an hour, Fernando. Please.

Fernando, looking pissed, storms out. Salvador follows him.

INT. FERNANDO'S ROOM – NIGHT

Fernando, still looking pissed, paces back and forth.

                      FERNANDO
          Motherfucker! Goddamn.

Salvador listens but doesn't say anything.

                      FERNANDO
          What good is it reserving the TV? Just tell
          me that. What good is it?

                      SALVADOR
          Calm down, man.

                      FERNANDO
          They haven't been here two weeks and
          they're already acting like they own the
          place.

Salvador doesn't answer. Fernando sits down on the bed and thinks for a moment.

                      FERNANDO
          What a bad time for Dad to die… And all
          because of that fucking truck driver. If I
          find him one day, he's gonna be one sorry
          son of a bitch.

Fernando sits there, furious, ruminating.

                    FERNANDO
          How about you turn on the radio to see
          how the game is going.

Salvador reaches out his hand to turn it on.

EXT. JUNKYARD – MORNING

Fernando enters the junkyard. He approaches Coyote, who is hammering on a dashboard.

                    FERNANDO
          What's up.

                    COYOTE
          What's up with you.

Fernando comes alongside him and watches him work.

                    FERNANDO
          What are you doing with that?

                    COYOTE
               (*concentrated, without looking up*)
          Straightening out this dashboard, thinking
          maybe I can sell it.

For a moment, neither speaks.

                    FERNANDO
               (*anxiously*)
          Did they bring in any more cars?

Coyote looks up and gestures toward one end of the junkyard.

                    COYOTE
          Six new ones. They're over there.

Fernando heads in that direction. El Coyote calls out to him.

> COYOTE
> Yo, Fernando… One of those cars that came in sounds like the one you been looking for.

El Coyote stands up and walks with him.

> COYOTE
> It's a Jetta that ran head on into a truck. Just like your dad's accident.

> FERNANDO
> Anyone die?

> COYOTE
> Just the driver…

Fernando looks at him, arches his eyebrows, and heads over to where the cars are. He is looking for the Jetta. The car is totally wrecked. Fernando looks through a broken window. The windshield has been smashed and there are tiny pieces of glass all over the car. Dried bloodstains cover the dashboard. The steering wheel is crushed up against the driver's seat. Part of the engine can be seen down next to the pedals. The front passenger seat is intact. Fernando circles the car, opens the passenger door, and slides in. He is grimacing, as if imagining the accident. He opens the glove compartment and removes some papers, toothpaste and a toothbrush. There is a single shoe on the floor. Fernando thinks for a moment, cocking his head to one side.

CUT TO

Fernando, looking downcast, walking in Coyote's direction.

> COYOTE
> Why you looking so blue?

FERNANDO
It's nothing, man.

COYOTE
It sucks, don't it?

Fernando nods. Coyote stops talking a moment to hammer on the dashboard.

COYOTE
You know what truck drivers say about accidents?

FERNANDO
What?

COYOTE
That the car that's gonna kill you has been on the road for the past ten hours.

FERNANDO
That's bullshit, Coyote.

FADE CUT

Fernando doesn't answer. He goes into the kitchen where Salvador is eating Jell–O at the table. He takes him by the arm.

FERNANDO
(*point-blank*)
How did my dad die?

SALVADOR
Oh, you wanna do this again?

FERNANDO
How did he die?

SALVADOR
I already told you: I don't remember.

FERNANDO
How the fuck don't you remember?

SALVADOR
I don't remember.

FERNANDO
Don't play around with me. Whose fault was it?

SALVADOR
I told you a thousand times.

FERNANDO
And you're gonna tell me a thousand more.

SALVADOR
Forget about it already...

INT. HOUSE – AFTERNOON

We see Fernando go into the house. Mercedes greets him.

MERCEDES
Hello.

FERNANDO
You're going to forget about it.

SALVADOR
(*fury in his eyes*)
Never.

Fernando gives him an ironic, half-smile.

                    FERNANDO
              That's what I wanted to hear.

INT. FERNANDO'S ROOM – DAY

Fernando is sleeping. There are voices and noise from outside the room. Fernando wakes up, opens the door and peeks over the staircase. He sees men carrying furniture. He runs downstairs and into his father's study.

INT. STUDY – MORNING

His mother is giving instructions to workers wearing gray uniforms and lifting belts.

                    FERNANDO
              What are you doing?

                    MOTHER
              We're going to turn this into a room for
              your sister.

                    FERNANDO
              She's not my sister.

                    MOTHER
              OK. A room for Paula.

                    FERNANDO
              But this is Dad's study!

                    MOTHER
              I know. But we need a room for her.

                    FERNANDO
              Why not leave her where she is?

MOTHER
That room's too small. Her stuff doesn't fit.

The mother turns to the workers.

MOTHER
Leave this desk over there, please.

Fernando stands in front of them.

MOTHER
What are you doing?

FERNANDO
Paula isn't going to sleep here. This is my dad's study.

MOTHER
I'm going to give you three seconds to move.

FERNANDO
You're in a real hurry to get married again, huh?

MOTHER
Don't start with this, Fernando.

FERNANDO
You really miss Dad, don't you.

MOTHER
(*hurt*)
Much more than you imagine.
(*snapping her fingers*)
Now, do me a favor and get out!

Fernando wants to say more but he hesitates. The workers look on, not sure what to do. Fernando opens his mouth to say something, perhaps to apologize, but his mother pushes him away.

                    MOTHER
  Get out.

INT. TV ROOM – NIGHT

Eduardo, Paula and Salvador are watching a soap opera. Eduardo has his arm around Paula and is stroking her neck. Salvador has his eye on them. Eduardo tries to kiss her but she turns her head away.

                    EDUARDO
  Are you mad about something?

Paula, her eyes glued to the television, points at the screen.

                    PAULA
  Hold on a sec. Joaquin is about to come in.

                    EDUARDO
  So?

                    PAULA
  Rosalba is inside and he's going to find
  out that she's cheating on him… Look!
  There he is.

Paula is totally fixated on the TV. Eduardo, looking annoyed, stands up.

                    EDUARDO
  I'm out of here.

                    PAULA
  Why, honey?

EDUARDO
It's late and I'm tired.

PAULA
Oh. All right... I'll go with you.

EDUARDO
No, that's OK, stay here.

Paula remains focused on the television.

PAULA
OK.

Eduardo taps Salvador's foot.

EDUARDO
See you around.

SALVADOR
See you.

Eduardo leaves. Salvador and Paula are left alone. Salvador has his eyes on Paula but she is glued to the TV.

SALVADOR
Don't you get bored?

Paula continues watching for a few seconds before turning toward him.

PAULA
I don't know. He's a nice guy. A little weird sometimes.

SALVADOR
Not Eduardo! The soap opera.

                    PAULA
                  (*laughing*)
          No way, man! It rocks.

                  SALVADOR
          Every time I see it, it's the same scene all
          over again.

                    PAULA
          Yeah, but that's life, right?

Salvador shrugs. The closing theme song plays. Paula stands up.

                    PAULA
          Yeah, see you tomorrow.

She approaches Salvador and gives him a kiss on the cheek.

                  SALVADOR
          Yeah, see you tomorrow.

Paula exits and Salvador starts counting to himself.

                  SALVADOR
          One, two, three, four, five, six, seven,
          eight, nine, ten, eleven, twelve, thirteen,
          fourteen, fifteen...

When he reaches fifteen, he jumps out and runs out to the garden.

EXT. GARDEN – NIGHT

Salvador tiptoes up to a window. The room is lit from the inside. Peeking in, he sees Paula undressing. She is tall and thin with a great figure. Naked, she looks at herself in the mirror for a moment. Salvador swallows and tries to catch his breath. Paula takes out a nightshirt and puts it on. She turns out the light.

FADE CUT

INT. KITCHEN – MORNING

Fernando, dressed in sports attire, is having a bowl of cereal for breakfast. Next to him, his mother is eating a papaya.

Salvador, still in pajamas and looking sleepy, is also at the table. He reaches for a banana in a fruit bowl in the middle of the table and just stops in mid-movement. His mother reaches over and pinches him.

> MOTHER
> Come on, sit up straight.

> SALVADOR
> Mom!

Salvador sits up. Fernando comes in with jeans and a t-shirt. He's just showered and his hair is damp. He makes a big show of greeting everyone.

> FERNANDO
> Good morning...

He opens the fridge, takes out a carton of milk, pours himself a glass and drinks it standing up. At the same time, he takes a section of the newspaper and starts reading.

> MOTHER
> Since I've got both of you here today: not this Saturday but the following Saturday, Claudio and I are going on a trip.

> SALVADOR
> Where?

                    MOTHER
To Spain. For two weeks.

                    SALVADOR
                    (*surprised*)
Two weeks?!

                    MOTHER
That's right, son, two weeks.

                    SALVADOR
That's not fair, Mom! My vacation is
almost over and I haven't gone anywhere.

                    MOTHER
Look, Salvador, sometimes vacations are
possible and sometimes they aren't.

                    SALVADOR
But why can't we all go?

Just as his mother is about to answer, Fernando butts in, without looking up from the paper.

                    FERNANDO
                    (*sarcastically*)
Give the lovebirds a chance. They barely
had a honeymoon.

                    MOTHER
Fernando!

                    CLAUDIO
                    (*irked*)
I'm going to Madrid for work and your
mom is coming with me like any good
wife would.

FERNANDO
(*lifting his hands as if
to prove his innocence*)
Don't get mad at me. I was defending you.

Claudio stops eating.

CLAUDIO
If you'll excuse me.

Pursing his lips, he leaves. Their mother stands up and looks at both of them.

MOTHER
This is the last time you make things difficult for me again.

She exits.

EXT. HOUSE/STREET – DAY

FADE CUT

Salvador opens the door to the house and starts walking down the street. Fernando exits and catches up to him.

FERNANDO
Salvador…

Salvador stops.

FERNANDO
I found him.

SALVADOR
Who?

FERNANDO
Lucio Estrada.

Salvador doesn't seem to understand.

>FERNANDO
>The fucking truck driver. I know where he lives.

>SALVADOR
>How do you know?

>FERNANDO
>I kept searching until I found him. I've been keeping track of him.

>SALVADOR
>I don't believe you.

>FERNANDO
>Dial 2-23-49, Piedras Negras, and see who answers the phone.

Salvador takes a few steps. Fernando reaches out for his shoulder and stops him.

>FERNANDO
>We'll head to Piedras Negras on Saturday afternoon, right after Mom and Claudio leave.

Salvador, serious, looks him right in the eye.

>SALVADOR
>For what?

>FERNANDO
>To kill him.

FADE CUT

EXT. GARDEN – AFTERNOON

It's a sunny afternoon and Paula is lying on a lounge chair in the garden. Salvador is next to her, sitting on the grass. They are listening to a CD player. Paula is wearing short shorts and a sleeveless top, leafing through a magazine. Salvador is pretending to read a magazine but actually staring at Paula's legs.

> SALVADOR
> Did you hear that my mom and your dad are going to Spain?

Paula puts down her magazine.

> SALVADOR
> (*after a beat*)
> Fernando and I are going on a trip together too.

> PAULA
> Where?

> SALVADOR
> Coahuila.

> PAULA
> Coahuila? What for?

> SALVADOR
> You know, just for fun…

> PAULA
> (*surprised*)
> Coahuila just for fun… That's weird. Did you ask them if you could?

> SALVADOR
> Nope. We're just going.

> PAULA
> Oh!... Now I get it.

They go back to reading their respective magazines. Paula seems to be reflecting on what Salvador has said.

> PAULA
> Listen... Can Eduardo and I tag along?

Salvador looks hesitant.

INT. FERNANDO'S ROOM – NIGHT

Salvador and Fernando are sitting on the bed.

> FERNANDO
> How much did you come up with?

> SALVADOR
> (*pulling a few hundred from his pants*)
> Three hundred was all I could get.

> FERNANDO
> Fuck. That's not going to be enough.

> SALVADOR
> How much you got?

> FERNANDO
> Fifteen hundred: all the money Mom deposited in my account. We'll spend that on gas alone.

> SALVADOR
> Whose car are we taking?

> FERNANDO
> Claudio's Suburban. We can sleep in the car.

Salvador pauses a moment before making his suggestion.

> SALVADOR
> Maybe Paula can help with the expenses.

> FERNANDO
> What? You told her?

> SALVADOR
> No! I just mentioned that we were going to Coahuila and she asked if she could come along. With Eduardo, that is.

> FERNANDO
> You're an asshole... Did you tell her why we were going?

> SALVADOR
> No way! I swear.

INT. TV ROOM – NIGHT

Fernando bursts into the TV room. Paula is lounging on the couch, watching TV.

> FERNANDO
> (*in a threatening tone*)
> You're not coming with us.

Paula arches her eyebrows without stirring.

> PAULA
> I'm not staying here by myself.

> FERNANDO
> So ask your little boyfriend over for a slumber party or go somewhere with him. But you're not going anywhere with us.

PAULA
Well, now I'm definitely going with you.

Fernando tries a more conciliatory strategy but keeps up the threatening tone.

FERNANDO
Listen, we're not going to a beach or to shop in San Antonio. We're going to take care of some business…

PAULA
What business?

FERNANDO
What the hell do you care?

PAULA
(*firmly but calmly*)
It's as simple as this, Fer – you don't take Eduardo and me with you, I'll make your life hell.

FERNANDO
Oh, I'm so scared…

PAULA
To start, I'll tell your mom about your little plan.

FERNANDO
I'm taking this trip whether my mom likes it or not. You get me?

Paula looks a little taken aback.

FERNANDO
So I don't give a shit what you do, sister.

                    PAULA
We'll see.

Fernando gives her a cocky smile and exits.

INT. DINING ROOM – DAY

The family is around the table eating lunch. Claudio is at the head of the table and their mother, next to him, is serving the food. The table is set with ceramic dishes and wooden salt and pepper shakers.

                    MOTHER
          Salvador, want more steak?

                    SALVADOR
          No thanks.

Paula hands out her dish to their mother.

                    PAULA
          I would, thanks.

Their mother puts more on her plate. Paula and Fernando glare at each other.

                    PAULA
               (to Mother)
          Maru, do you know what Fernando and
          Salvador told me?

                    MOTHER
          What?

                    PAULA
               (looking straight at Fernando)
          That they're planning a little trip.

Salvador can't believe she's announcing their plans.

MOTHER
(*to Fernando*)
Oh, is that right? Where to?

Fernando is about to answer when Paula interrupts.

PAULA
Somewhere up north, isn't that right?

Fernando looks at her, furious. Now the mother looks furious as well.

MOTHER
What for?

FERNANDO
We're going to Querétaro to visit some friends.

MOTHER
You're lying. Why wouldn't you have told me?

PAULA
(*with a cocky smile*)
The thing is, they asked me to ask for permission because they want me and Eduardo to go along.

MOTHER
Well, I don't know…

CLAUDIO
When were you planning on going?

PAULA
On Sunday. We'll be back Friday.

Fernando and Salvador are totally floored by this turn of events. Claudio nods.

> CLAUDIO
> That doesn't sound like a bad idea. But I'm not thrilled about Eduardo going.

> PAULA
> Oh, Dad! We're not going to get into any trouble.

> CLAUDIO
> OK, fine with me.

Fernando, Salvador and Paula exchange glances. She smiles.

INT. TV ROOM – NIGHT

Paula is watching television. Salvador comes in and sits down. He watches TV for a moment before speaking.

> SALVADOR
> What's the story here?

> PAULA
> Jorge knows that something's up between Rosalba and the brother.

> SALVADOR
> (*surprised*)
> Rosalba's brother?!

> PAULA
> No, no: Jorge's brother.

They watch a bit more. Salvador wants to get back to the real topic.

SALVADOR
Fernando asked me to convince you not to come.

PAULA
And?

SALVADOR
The thing is, we're going someplace far, Paula.

PAULA
So you don't want me to go either, huh?

SALVADOR
I do, but the thing is… You'd be bored.

PAULA
More bored than I am here? Hard to believe.

SALVADOR
You and Eduardo would be better off going to Cuernavaca or something else… We'll vouch for you.

PAULA
No. I want to go someplace new, someplace I've never been. I'm sick of Acapulco, Valle de Bravo, Cancún… All the same old places.

SALVADOR
Yeah, the thing is, this is a really long trip, and you're not going to like what we're going there for.

Paula looks him straight in the eye.

                    PAULA
And what's that?

                    SALVADOR
Nothing.

                    PAULA
So then I'm coming.

Paula goes back to the television. Salvador looks anxious.

EXT. STREET – DAY

A taxi is outside the house. The driver puts the luggage in the trunk.

                    MOTHER
              (*saying goodbye to Paula*)
          Be good, sweetie, and look out for the
          boys.

                    PAULA
I will, Maru, don't worry.

                    MOTHER
                 (*to the boys*)
          And you two: be good.

She kisses them. Claudio approaches and hugs Paula.

                    CLAUDIO
          See you soon, honey.
              (*turning to the boys and patting them
                  each on the back*)
          You guys are in charge, OK?

They both nod. Claudio and the mom get into the taxi and drive off.

                    FERNANDO
                    (*to Paula*)
We're leaving at 4:30, whether you're ready or not.

Paula pulls some keys from her pants pocket and presses a button. The Suburban beeps, indicating the alarm is on.

                    PAULA
            Sure thing. Whenever you're ready.

EXT. HOUSE – AFTERNOON

The Suburban is parked outside the house. Paula and Salvador put in luggage, kitchen utensils, a cooler. Eduardo drives up in a sports car and parks it. He approaches and Paula embraces him. Salvador watches, looking a little jealous.

                    PAULA
    Ready?

                    EDUARDO
    Ready.

Eduardo puts his suitcase into the car. Fernando comes out with his hand wrapped in a sweater.

                    FERNANDO
    Let's go.

Eduardo approaches the driver's side but Fernando stops him.

                    FERNANDO
    I'll drive.

                    EDUARDO
        OK, take it easy.

Eduardo and Paula get in the back. Fernando gets into the car and pulls a pistol from inside the sweater. He hands it to Salvador and whispers.

>   FERNANDO
>   Put this under the seat.

Salvador can't believe it. He wants to say something but Fernando now hisses at him.

>   FERNANDO
>   Hide it. Now.

Paula and Eduardo are oblivious. Salvador hides the gun. Fernando starts the car and they drive off.

EXT. HIGHWAY TOLLBOOTH – AFTERNOON

They stop at a tollbooth and then speed off down the highway.

INT. SUV – AFTERNOON

Fernando has his eyes on the road. Salvador checks out the landscape. In the back seat, Eduardo and Paula giggle and play around.

EXT. HIGHWAY – AFTERNOON

The SUV continues down the highway. It's raining.

INT. SUV – AFTERNOON

Fernando turns on the windshield wipers. Eduardo touches Paula's breast and, laughing, she pushes him away. Fernando sees this in the rearview mirror and turns his attention back to the road. He turns on the radio and finds a station.

> PAULA
> Leave that song on, please.

> FERNANDO
> I don't like this song.

> PAULA
> (*smiling at Eduardo,
> who is caressing her*)
> Please don't change it. It's a classic!

Paula and Eduardo sing and shake to the rhythm of a catchy hit. As soon as the song has ended, Fernando searches the dial for another song but not finding one he likes, he turns off the radio. Paula and Eduardo are now making out. Salvador watches them out of the corner of his eye.

EXT. HIGHWAY EXIT TO QUERÉTARO – AFTERNOON

The SUV takes the exit to Querétaro.

INT. SUV – AFTERNOON

Fernando continues concentrating on the road. Eduardo and Paula are no longer making out. Salvador spots a "motel" sign and turns the wheel.

EXT. MOTEL – DUSK

The SUV pulls up in front of the motel. It's raining out.

> EDUARDO
> Why we stopping here?

> FERNANDO
> We'll spend the night here.

                    EDUARDO
            Why not keep driving?

                    FERNANDO
            I don't see too good at night.

                    EDUARDO
            I can drive then.

                    FERNANDO
            That's all right, dude.

Paula cleans off the window. The place looks pretty rundown.

                    PAULA
            This is where we are going to stay?

                    FERNANDO
            We can't afford a more expensive place.

                    EDUARDO
            But this place is a shithole! Seriously?

                    FERNANDO
            What were you hoping for? Five stars?

                    EDUARDO
            Only because they don't do six.

Eduardo chuckles at his own joke but Paula barely cracks a smile.

                    EDUARDO
                    (*to Salvador*)
            You guys don't have any money, for real?

                    SALVADOR
            We have a little.

                    EDUARDO
          Listen, man. I'll pay for the hotel, but let's
          go someplace decent. What do you say?

                    FERNANDO
          We don't need you to pay for anything.

                    EDUARDO
          Just tonight. I'm like waving the white
          scarf, OK?

EXT. FIVE-STAR HOTEL IN QUERÉTARO – NIGHT

The SUV pulls up in front of a nice hotel. A bellboy with an umbrella comes running up to keep them dry. While the others run toward the lobby, Paula turns from under the umbrella and pushes the button to put on the car alarm.

INT. HOTEL LOBBY – NIGHT

The four go into the lobby. The men shake themselves off. Eduardo approaches the reception with a worldly air. A young and perky woman in a light brown uniform is waiting.

                    RECEPTIONIST
          Good evening.

                    EDUARDO
          Good evening. Good evening.

                    PAULA
          Three rooms, please.

Eduardo turns toward her, miffed. He smiles for the sake of the receptionist and turns his attention back to her.

                    EDUARDO
          Two doubles, please.

                    PAULA
        Three rooms, please.

Eduardo turns back to her, takes her by the arm, and leads her out of earshot.

                    EDUARDO
        What's up with you?

                    PAULA
        So that's why you wanted to come? To see
        if we would have sex?

                    EDUARDO
        No. But I don't see the problem in…

                    PAULA
            (*interrupting*)
        You never see things my way.

                    EDUARDO
        All right, all right.
            (*heading back to the receptionist*)
        Three rooms. One double and two singles.

INT. HOTEL ROOM – NIGHT

Salvador and Fernando are in the room. Sitting on the bed, Fernando takes off his shirt. Salvador pulls a few things from his suitcase.

                    FERNANDO
        Goddamn, man, why did you tell her to
        come?

                    SALVADOR
        We got something good out of it, right?
        A free hotel!

FERNANDO
She just came to fool around with her boyfriend.

SALVADOR
Did you see how that played out, though? She stopped him in his tracks.

Fernando undresses and puts on his pajamas. Salvador studies him a moment, thinking.

SALVADOR
So what's the gun for?

Fernando ignores him and turns down the bed covers. He sees that his brother is waiting for a response.

FERNANDO
What do you think it's for?

SALVADOR
Yeah, but…

FERNANDO
You gonna chicken out?

SALVADOR
I never chicken out.

Fernando gets into bed and Salvador, who is still dressed, heads for the door.

FERNANDO
Where you going?

SALVADOR
To get a Coke.

FERNANDO
Don't take too long, man.

Salvador exits the hotel room and walks down a hall. He glances up at the numbers of the other rooms and we see him mentally counting his steps.

EXT. HOTEL GARDEN – NIGHT

Salvador reaches the garden. It's still pouring out. He finds a path that takes him past the back of the rooms. Counting his steps, he approaches a window on tiptoe. He sees Eduardo sitting on his bed and talking on the phone. He crouches down, walks a few more steps and spies into a half–open curtain of the next room. Paula is pacing the room and talking on the phone. She seems to be arguing. She throws the phone down and looks out the window. Salvador crouches down. The phone rings and Paula answers. Salvador peeks into the window again. Paula yells something else into the phone and hangs up. She paces the room like a caged tiger. The phone rings again, but this time she doesn't answer. She starts getting undressed, taking off her blouse and bra. Salvador starts to breathe audibly. Paula turns toward the window. Salvador crouches down quickly. Paula closes the curtain and the phone rings again. Disappointed, Salvador moves away from the window and sees Eduardo in the next room, talking on the hotel phone.

INT. HOTEL ROOM – NIGHT

Salvador enters the hotel room, soaking wet. The lights in the room are off and he enters on tiptoe to avoid waking Fernando. He heads into the bathroom, closes the door and turns on the light. Looking into the mirror, he sees the water running down his face. He takes off his shirt and contemplates a large scar across his chest.

EXT. HOTEL PARKING LOT – DAWN

The three young men are next to the SUV, their luggage on the ground. Paula comes out and turns off the car alarm. Fernando, looking annoyed, opens the back.

INT. SUV – AFTERNOON

Fernando is driving. In the back seat, Paula and Eduardo are sitting apart from each other and not speaking. Fernando turns on the radio. Fiddling with the dial, he finds the hit song from the previous day. He leaves in on for a while and checks the rearview mirror for the couple's reaction. Seeing them both miffed, he smiles and changes to another station.

EXT. HIGHWAY – DAY

Shots of the SUV driving across different landscapes.

INT. SUV – DAY

They are parked at the side of the road. Through the window we can see Eduardo looking for a place to pee.

>   FERNANDO
>   (*to Salvador*)
>   Where did you two stop for gas?
>
>   SALVADOR
>   Who do you mean by "you two"?
>
>   FERNANDO
>   Who do you think I mean? You and my
>   dad.
>
>   SALVADOR
>   I don't remember.

FERNANDO
You don't remember?

SALVADOR
No!

FERNANDO
Well, you need to remember, OK?
Everything: where you ate, where you
slept, where you stopped to pee.

Salvador turns his face to the window, annoyed. Paula furrows her brow, not understanding what this is about.

EXT. HIGHWAY – DAY

The SUV continues down the highway. At one intersection, the cops are doing a stop and search. The cars ahead of them are already stopped and the cops are searching them.

FERNANDO
(to Salvador)
Hand me the gun. Now.

Salvador reaches around under the seat.

SALVADOR
Why? What's going on?

FERNANDO
Just give it to me!

Salvador pulls out the gun and Fernando practically rips it out of his hand. Fernando turns to Paula.

FERNANDO
Hide this under your clothes.

PAULA
Are you crazy? What the hell?

FERNANDO
Hide it or we're all going to jail.

EDUARDO
(*to Paula*)
Toss it out the window.

FERNANDO
Don't be an idiot. You think they won't see that?

Paula tucks the gun in her pants beneath her blouse. They slowly approach the stop. Fernando takes a handful of bullets from his pockets and hands them to Paula.

FERNANDO
This too.

Paula hides them in her pocket. An officer comes over. Fernando opens the window.

POLICEMAN
Where you headed?

FERNANDO
(*playing it cool*)
Coahuila.

The POLICEMAN peaks into the window.

POLICEMAN
What are you going there for?

FERNANDO
We're visiting an aunt.

POLICEMAN
What city?

FERNANDO
Nuevo Laredo.

POLICEMAN
(*a suspicious look on his face*)
Make up your mind, kid. You going to Tamaulipas or Cohuila?

Fernando opens his mouth to answer but the officer interrupts him.

POLICEMAN
Pull off to the side, please.

EDUARDO
(*murmuring*)
Idiot.

Fernando parks the car. Another two officers approach.

POLICEMAN
I need all of you to step out of the vehicle, please.

All four get out of the SUV. The second policeman enters the SUV and gropes beneath the seats. The third policeman opens the back of the SUV and checks the luggage.

EDUARDO
You looking for some criminal?

POLICEMAN
Nope, just a routine check. Put your hands on the vehicle.

All four do as they're told. The policeman pats them down but when he gets to Paula, he just shrugs.

> POLICEMAN
> You're good, little lady.

> POLICEMAN TWO
> Nothing to report here, officer.

> POLICEMAN
> All right, kids, you're good to go.

Looking nervous, the four of them get back into the SUV. The policeman waves them on. Fernando drives back onto the highway.

EXT. HIGHWAY – DAY

The car makes its way down the highway, leaving the police behind.

INT. SUV – AFTERNOON

They all look afraid. Fernando breaks the silence.

> FERNANDO
> Give me back the gun.

> EDUARDO
> Don't give him a damn thing.

> FERNANDO
> Give it to me!

Paula takes the gun from her pants and examines it.

> PAULA
> This is my dad's.

FERNANDO
Just give it to me!

PAULA
What do you want it for?

SALVADOR
In case we get jumped.

Paula has her eyes on Salvador, who looks the other way.

PAULA
That's a lie.

FERNANDO
(*exasperated*)
Give it to me. Now.

EDUARDO
What the hell do you two have planned?

FERNANDO
What the hell do you care?

EDUARDO
You guys are both acting pretty damn strange, you know?

FERNANDO
I don't give a fuck.
(*to Paula*)
Give me the gun, goddamn it.

Paula continues holding the weapon. Eduardo tries to pull it from her hand but she doesn't let go. Fernando slams on the brakes.

EDUARDO
Throw it out the window.

Paula starts rolling down her window. Salvador turns back toward her.

> SALVADOR
> (*conciliatory*)
> How about you give it to me? Please.

Hearing the tone of Salvador's voice, Paula hesitates and then hands the gun over to him, along with the bullets. Salvador puts the gun back under the seat and hands the bullets to Fernando, who tucks them away. After a moment of silence, Eduardo speaks.

> EDUARDO
> We'll get off at San Luis Potosi.

> PAULA
> Why?

> EDUARDO
> What do you mean, "why?" Don't you realize that these...

> FERNANDO
> These what, asshole?

> EDUARDO
> I'm not going to argue with you. You're screwed up.

Fernando slams on the brakes a second and then accelerates.

> EDUARDO
> See what I'm saying? You're crazy.

Fernando slams on the brakes, then hits the gas again.

EDUARDO
(*snapping his fingers*)
Let us off here... Now.

Fernando pulls the SUV abruptly off the road and stops.

FERNANDO
(*snapping his fingers*)
Get out. Now.

Eduardo gets out of the car, walks around to the other side and opens Paula's door.

EDUARDO

Let's go.

PAULA

No.

EDUARDO
I said, let's go, dammit!

PAULA

No!

EDUARDO
(*surprised*)

What?

PAULA
I'm staying with them.

EDUARDO
(*twirling his index finger near his temple*)
This guy's nuts. Out of his mind.

SALVADOR
All right, dude, just go already.

                    EDUARDO
          Who are you to tell me where to go?
          Bratty little kid.
                    (to Paula)
          You coming or not?

Paula shakes her head. His face red with fury, Eduardo takes his things and closes the back of the SUV. Fernando burns rubber as they drive off, leaving Eduardo alone at the side of the road. Inside the vehicle, no one speaks. Suddenly, Fernando pulls off to the side of the road again.

                    FERNANDO
          You can still get out.

                    PAULA
          If anyone should get out, it's you. This
          is my dad's truck and you're packing my
          dad's gun.

                    FERNANDO
          Are you getting out or not?

                    PAULA
          Nope. Because I don't want to.

                    FERNANDO
          Well, you're responsible for whatever
          happens.

EXT. HIGHWAY – DAY

Shots of the SUV driving down the highway. We see the car pull up to a dingy roadside restaurant. The three get out of the Suburban and head in.

INT. ROADSIDE RESTAURANT – DAY

The place is small. There is a truck parked right outside. Two truck drivers are eating at one of the tables. Paula, Fernando and Salvador sit at a table in the back. A FAT GUY brings over three menus.

>FAT GUY
>What are you drinking?

>FERNANDO
>A beer for me, whatever you got.

>SALVADOR
>Coke.

>PAULA
>A cappuccino for me, please.

The fat guy furrows his eyebrows.

>FAT GUY
>A what? Sorry.

>FERNANDO
>(*rolling his eyes at Paula*)
>Coffee with milk.

The fat guy heads back into the kitchen. Salvador takes a newspaper from the next table and starts reading it while Salvador and Paula check out the menu.

>FERNANDO
>(*to Paula, without looking up from the paper*)
>How much money you got with you?

Paula takes the wallet from her purse and counts it under the table.

PAULA
Enough.

Fernando yanks the wallet from her. Paula tries to get it back but Fernando won't give it to her.

PAULA
Give that back to me, asshole.

Fernando takes some bills from the wallet.

FERNANDO
Two hundred and fifty. Got any more?

PAULA
(*firmly*)
No!

FERNANDO
What about credit cards?

PAULA
No. I left them back in the city. Now give me my money.

FERNANDO
It's for the pool, you get me? That is, if you want to stick with us.

Paula is about to protest but Salvador intervenes.

SALVADOR
We don't have very much, Paula.

PAULA
And no credit card?

                    FERNANDO
We don't have a daddy to give us an
extension on his.

EXT. HIGHWAY – DUSK

The sun is going down. The SUV pulls up in front of a
rundown hotel. A neon sign contrasts with the outlines of
the cactus against the red evening sky. The three enter the
lobby. A WOMAN WITH DYED HAIR is listening to a
radio that rests on the counter.

                    FERNANDO
How much for a room?

                    WOMAN
You looking to stay a few hours or the
whole night?

                    FERNANDO
The night.

                    WOMAN
Fifty.

                    FERNANDO
We'll take one room.

                    PAULA
Two rooms, he means.

Fernando sneers at her.

                    FERNANDO
Honey, we don't have enough for two
rooms: or you wanna sleep out in the truck?

Paula sticks her hand in the back pocket of her pants and
pulls out a hundred.

                    PAULA
            I'll pay for it myself.

                  FERNANDO
            Now you get to pay for both of them.

The woman takes the hundred and hands them keys, both with a clunky wooden keychain.

                    WOMAN
            Rooms 8 and 13.

INT. MOTEL ROOM – NIGHT

Paula enters the room. There's a queen-size bed with a ratty coverlet, a small chest of drawers with peeling paint and a bare light bulb hanging from the ceiling. Paula looks disgusted. She puts her suitcase on the mattress, which bends a little under the weight. She enters the bathroom and turns on the light. A cockroach comes out from behind the door and Paula gasps. The toilet has no cover. Paula flushes and heads back to the bedroom. Pulling down the coverlet, she sees the raggedy sheet covering the mattress. She takes three blouses from her suitcase and uses them to cover the bed. Turning off the light, she lies down on top of the clothing.

INT. MOTEL ROOM – DAWN

Paula is fast asleep. Shouting can be heard O.S. Paula opens her eyes and listens.

                  WOMAN (O.S.)
            No, no...

Paula gets out of back and walks to the window. She opens the curtain and sees a tall man wearing typical farmer's clothes beating a woman who is on the ground, trying to defend herself.

                           MAN
         You're a whore, that's what you are…

Paula is frightened but cannot look away. She makes no
attempt to intervene. The man pulls the woman up and
punches her. Bleeding, she falls to the ground with a thud.
Looking up, he discovers Paula spying on them, fury in his
eyes. Paula gasps. The man takes a step toward the window.
From the ground, the woman pulls a switchblade. She
stands up and stabs his shoulder. Now he turns back toward
her, striking her, and she drops the switchblade.

                           MAN
         Little bitch…

He grabs her by the hair and drags her to a 1971 Dodge
pickup.

                         WOMAN
         Let go of me, Joaquin, please…

He strikes her across the face again and tosses her into the
front seat. The truck takes off. Paula watches it go. She stares
out the window a moment longer and then heads outside.
On the ground, she discovers the switchblade. She picks it
up – it's covered in blood. She hears someone approaching
from behind and, startled, turns around. It's Fernando,
who is just a few feet away. Salvador is watching from the
doorway. An old farmer type is watching them from the
other door. Paula doesn't drop the switchblade.

                        FERNANDO
         What a beating, huh? He almost killed her.

Paula, still in shock, nods.

                        FERNANDO
         It must have been his wife. Or maybe a
         prostitute, who knows?

Salvador approaches them. The older man closes the door.

> SALVADOR
> (*pointing toward the switchblade*)
> What do you want that for?

Paula examines the switchblade, which catches the light for a second. Her hand is stained with blood.

> PAULA
> I know don't, maybe I'll need it...

Fernando comes over and gets a closer look.

> FERNANDO
> Nice little souvenir from the trip, huh?

Salvador smiles and so does Paula. Fernando pulls on Salvador's arm.

> FERNANDO
> Let's go back to bed...

Paula heads back into her room.

INT. MOTEL ROOM – NIGHT

Paula washes the switchblade in the sink. Drops of blood mixed with water drip onto the tiles. When she is finished, Paula dries the switchblade on the towel and then opens and closes it a few times.

FADE CUT

INT. SUBURBAN – MORNING

Fernando is driving while Salvador looks out the window. In the back seat, Paula looks pensive.

PAULA
Where are we going?

SALVADOR
(*tired of repeating it*)
Coahuila.

PAULA
I know that. But what for?

Salvador is going to answer when Fernando interrupts.

FERNANDO
To buy 200 pounds of marijuana.

Paula is dumbstruck. Salvador laughs and then she does do.

PAULA
For real.

They are driving past what appears to be a general store.

Fernando puts on the brakes, pulls off the road and drives in reverse. He pulls out a fifty and hands it to Salvador.

FERNANDO
Buy three cans of sardines, if they got 'em, and some sandwich bread. If they don't have that, get whatever you want.

Salvador gets out of the SUV and heads to the shop. Fernando turns back to Paula and finally answers her question.

FERNANDO
We're going to the place where my dad was killed.

PAULA
Was he killed in Coahuila?

FERNANDO
Yeah. Didn't you know?

PAULA
No. Your mom told us he died in a car crash but she didn't say where or when or how.

FERNANDO
The crash was about 120 miles outside of Piedras Negras.

PAULA
Is that far from here?

FERNANDO
Twelve or thirteen hours.

PAULA
That far?

FERNANDO
You can head back if you want.

PAULA
I already said no. And don't even think about leaving me on the side of the road.

Fernando cracks a grin. Salvador comes back with a bunch of junk food. He puts the packages on the seat.

FERNANDO
That all they got?

SALVADOR
No… They had powdered milk. You want me to buy some?

FERNANDO
Nah man. Let's go.

EXT. HIGHWAY – DAY

The Suburban makes its way down the highway.

INT. SUBURBAN – AFTERNOON

Paula is falling asleep. They drive past some women and children. There are rattlesnake carcasses hung up on a stick. Some of the women are carrying live eagles and squirrels.

SALVADOR
(*his eyes widening*)
That's the place! That's where we stopped.

Fernando pulls over and Paula wakes up.

PAULA
What is it?

A woman comes rushing over to the car, followed by three or four kids dressed in torn, ragged clothes. Fernando rolls down his window.

WOMAN
Eagles for sale! Real cheap.

KIDS
Toss us a few coins for a soda!

Fernando gets out of the car. Paula and Salvador both open their car doors. The children crowd around them.

FERNANDO
Why did you guys stop here?

Salvador points to the hanging snake carcasses.

                    SALVADOR
        Dad bought a snake.

                    FERNANDO
        A snake?

                    SALVADOR
        Yup. To eat. He said it cleans out your
        blood.

                    WOMAN
        That's right, son. And it cures cancer and
        achy bones.

Crowded by the kids, Fernando pulls out some spare change and hands it over. Paula pulls out a ten–peso bill and hands it over. Fernando looks at her, a little surprised. The woman yanks at Fernando's arm and he goes over to see the snakes. A little boy approaches Paula and shows her a squirrel tied with a little rope.

                    BOY
        Miss, wouldn't you like him?

Paula strikes the squirrel's head.

                    PAULA
        How much?

                    BOY
        Fifteen.

Paula pulls money from her pocket and pays him.

INT. SUBURBAN – AFTERNOON

Salvador is holding the dead rattlesnake. Paula, the live squirrel. Salvador takes a bite of the snake and starts chewing. He pulls off a chunk and offers Fernando.

> SALVADOR
> Want some?

Fernando looks over and shakes his head. Paula perks up.

> PAULA
> I want some!

Salvador hands the chunk to her and Paula chews it slowly.

> PAULA
> It tastes like dried shrimp.

Salvador smiles. Paula holds the squirrel up to him.

> PAULA
> What should we call him?

Salvador is going to answer when Fernando interrupts.

> FERNANDO
> Cecilia. That's the name of the girl he likes.

> SALVADOR
> Shut up. That's not true.

> PAULA
> Cecilia. I like it. Let's call her that.

EXT. HIGHWAY – DAY

The Suburban makes its way across the desert.

INT. SUV – AFTERNOON

Fernando pulls off to the side of the road and brings the SUV to a stop. He looks tired.

SALVADOR
What are we going to do?

FERNANDO
I'm going to sleep. Don't know about the two of you.

Paula leans toward the front seat.

PAULA
I can drive in the meantime.

Fernando looks back at her, a sneer on his face.

FERNANDO
You? How many times you driven on the highway?

PAULA
Like, ten times in Cuernavaca.

FERNANDO
(*sneering*)
How many times?

PAULA
(*pissed*)
Why are you such a dick sometimes?

FERNANDO
Amen! The little lady says bad words.

PAULA
I just don't get it. You were being cool for a while and now you act like a jerk again. I think you're messed up.

                    FERNANDO
Well, that's me. What're you going to do
about it?

                    SALVADOR
Cut it out, Fernando. She was just trying
to help.

                    FERNANDO
And I said she can't.

Fernando jumps into the back seat and lies down.

                    FERNANDO
Good night.

INT. SUV – AFTERNOON

Fernando is sleeping in the back seat. Paula and Salvador are listening to the radio in the front seat. Paula is stroking Cecilia.

                    PAULA
What do they eat?

                    SALVADOR
Who knows? Bread, seeds… Are you
going to let her go?

                    PAULA
Cecilia?
                    (smiling)
No. I'm keeping her.

Paula turns the dial from station to station. Suddenly Salvador stops her.

                    SALVADOR
Leave that on!

                    PAULA
                (*surprised*)
        But it sounds like elevator music.

                  SALVADOR
        No... It's the Monterrey Rancherita!

                    PAULA
        What?

                  SALVADOR
        The Rancherita... My dad used to say
        they listen to it as far south as Guatemala.
        That was our music when we'd go on
        road trips.

                    PAULA
        Your dad liked this music?

                  SALVADOR
        Oh, yeah, a ton.

Fernando sits up and glares at them.

                  FERNANDO
        Who can sleep with you two yip–
        yapping?

EXT. HIGHWAY – DAY

The Suburban pulls back onto the road. A truck coming up on them honks its horn. Fernando checks the rearview mirror and swears.

                  FERNANDO
        Fucker!

INT. HIGHWAY – DUSK

The SUV makes its way across the flat dry landscape.

>   FERNANDO
>   (to Paula, who is falling asleep
>   in the back seat)
>   Give me an apple, would you?

>   PAULA
>   Why?

>   FERNANDO
>   Because I'm hungry.

>   PAULA
>   (catty)
>   Learn to say PLEASE.

She points her finger at him.

>   FERNANDO
>   Over there...
>   (Paula looks and Fernando
>   points with his finger)
>   Not there... Over there.

Suddenly, an animal crosses the highway and Salvador gasps.

>   SALVADOR
>   Look out!

The SUV strikes the animal (we still don't know what it is). Fernando loses control of the SUV, which spins off the highway, right into a flock of goats. Finally, the SUV stops. The air is filled with dust and several of the goats are dead. A young SHEPHERD (about 10 years old) watches in disbelief from beneath a tree.

                    FERNANDO
            What was that?

Salvador's breath is raspy. Paula is speechless.

                    FERNANDO
            You guys OK?

The dust settles slowly. Fernando soberly examines the scene.

                    FERNANDO
            Goddamn it!

Salvador turns around to look at the dead goats. Fernando tries to start the SUV to drive off. Salvador yells at him.

                    SALVADOR
            No!

Fernando continues. Salvador pulls the keys from the ignition.

                    SALVADOR
            No, dammit, you're not running away.

Fernando takes a deep breath. Paula gets out of the SUV and heads to the shepherd, who starts to sob. Fernando also gets out of the car. One of the goats is bleating. Fernando turns back toward the highway and sees a dog with broken legs lying in the middle of the road.

                    SHEPHERD
                    (to Paula)
            My goats... I'm going to be in big
            trouble...

                    PAULA
            It's going to be all right. Don't cry...

Fernando walks over to the dog. He passes a goat that is bleating, wounded. Fernando is spooked by the sound. The dog whimpers. Fernando reaches the dog and, being as careful as possible, pulls him to the side of the road. The movement hurts the dog, who tries to bite Fernando. Salvador approaches and gives him a hand. A truck passes on the other side of the highway.

>> SHEPHERD (O.S.)
> My goats... My goats...

Fernando looks around: three or four goats are trotting nervously amidst a half dozen carcasses. The wounded goat bleats loudly. Paula, kneeling down, tries to calm down the young shepherd.

>> PAULA
> Don't worry. We'll pay you for them.

The shepherd continues sobbing. Fernando looks down at his hands. They are covered with the dog's blood. Salvador, his brow furrowed, sits down on a rock.

>> FERNANDO
>> (*to himself*)
> Goddamn it!

Fernando walks toward the SUV, sees one of the tires is flat, and kicks it. He gets into the car, looks under the seat, and pulls out the gun. Resolved, he walks over to the wounded goat. He lifts the gun and points it at the goat's head but he can't bring himself to pull the trigger. The goat looks at him, its eyes bulging, and bleats again. Fernando tucks the pistol into his belt.

EXT. DESERT – DUSK

The boy is walking down a path. Paula, Fernando and Salvador follow behind him. They come to an adobe house.

An old man missing his right arm is cutting branches with a machete. When he sees them, he stops what he's going.

>					FERNANDO
> Afternoon.

>					OLD MAN
> Afternoon.
>					(*to the boy*)
> What happened?

Fernando answers for him.

>					FERNANDO
> We had an accident and well… We ran over the goats.

The old man, angry, turns to the boy.

>					OLD MAN
> You damn kid! How many times I gotta tell you not to let them graze near the highway?

>					PAULA
> Don't blame him. It was our fault.

The boy's chin trembles.

>					FERNANDO
> We'll pay you for the goats and for the dog too.

>					OLD MAN
>					(*to the boy*)
> Which of the dogs?

>					BOY
> "El Mocho."

The old man shakes his head.

> FERNANDO
> The dog might live.

> OLD MAN
> Where is he?

EXT. PLACE OF THE ACCIDENT – EVENING

Fernando, Salvador and the old man reach the spot of the accident. The old man examines one of the dead goats. The goat that was wounded and bleating is now dead. When the dog sees the old man approach, he starts to whimper. The old man approaches, looks the dog over, lifts the machete, and brings it down onto the dog. The dog lets out a final cry. Fernando cringes. The old man puts the machete back onto his belt, approaches one of the dead goats and lifts it over his shoulder.

> OLD MAN
> Help me carry them.

EXT. ADOBE HOUSE – EVENING

Fernando and the old man approach with the goats, followed by Salvador, who is panting from the exertion of carrying the carcasses. The living goats follow behind. Paula and the boy are waiting for them.

> OLD MAN
> *(to the boy)*
> Lock up the goats, go on.

The boy gathers the goats and leads them into a corral made of branches. Fernando, looking woeful, approaches the old man.

FERNANDO
How much do I owe you for the goats?

The old man shrugs.

OLD MAN
Whatever you want to give me.

FERNANDO
No. How much? You tell me.

OLD MAN
Well, it would be forty per goat.

Fernando pulls out some bills and hands them over to the old man.

FERNANDO
I got three hundred.

OLD MAN
Why that much?

FERNANDO
It's two hundred for the goats and a hundred for the dog.

The old man hands him back the last hundred.

OLD MAN
Don't worry about it. That dog was a mutt. I'll get myself another one.

Fernando won't accept the bill. He gestures for the man to keep it.

OLD MAN
OK, young man… Listen, at least have a cup of coffee before you go.

INT. ADOBE HOUSE – EVENING

They enter the humble adobe house. It has a table with three chairs, a wood-burning stove and a few mats. An elderly white-skinned woman (90 or so) is sitting in a rocking chair in front of the TV.

> OLD MAN
> I'm home, Ma.

The old woman turns to them but her pupils are cloudy. She is blind.

> OLD LADY
> Who's there with you?

> OLD MAN
> A few kids who got into an accident off the highway.
> *(to Paula and Salvador)*
> Sit down, please.

Paula sits on a rickety chair and Salvador continues to stand, staring at the television as if confused by something.

> SALVADOR
> Do you have electricity?

The old man chuckles.

> OLD MAN
> No kid. I hook up the TV to the truck battery.
> *(to Fernando and Salvador)*
> Sit down. Make yourselves at home.

> FERNANDO
> We'll be there in a minute. We're going to change the tire on the SUV and we'll be back.

Fernando takes Salvador by the arm and pulls him out of the house. Paula opens her mouth but Fernando is already out the door.

> FERNANDO
> We won't be long.

They exit.

EXT. DESERT/PLACE OF THE ACCIDENT – NIGHT

Fernando and Salvador are crouched down, trying to figure out how to change the tire. Fernando straightens up.

> SALVADOR
> Fernando…

Fernando, who continues working, responds.

> FERNANDO
> What is it?

> SALVADOR
> Are we really going to find Lucio Estrada?

Fernando stops what he is doing and turns to look at his brother, nodding solemnly.

> SALVADOR
> And what are we going to do when we find him?

> FERNANDO
> Kick the shit out of him.

> SALVADOR
> Are you thinking of killing him?

FERNANDO
Well, he killed my dad, didn't he?

Salvador nods and gazes out toward the highway. A truck rumbles by and he watches it pass.

FERNANDO
What do you want to do?

SALVADOR
I don't know.

FERNANDO
You're gonna chicken out, aren't you?

SALVADOR
No, man, it's not that… It's just…

FERNANDO
What is it?

SALVADOR
No… Nothing.

They are silent for a moment, each lost in thought. Fernando gets back to work on the tire.

INT. ADOBE HOUSE – NIGHT

PAULA is sitting down at the table. The old man and the boy are sitting with her. She's drinking from a mug.

PAULA
What time is it?

OLD MAN
Must be about nine-thirty.

PAULA
They're sure taking a while…

OLD MAN
Fixing that tire must've taken them longer than they thought.

The music from Paula's soap opera is playing. Paula stands and approaches the old woman.

PAULA
You watch "On the Edge of Love" too?

OLD LADY
(*turns toward Paula, chuckling*)
I listen to it.

PAULA
(*embarrassed*)
Sorry.

The characters on TV start talking. The old woman turns her ear toward the television and no one in the room speaks.

OLD LADY
What's happening?

PAULA
Rosalba is making out with Martin. They don't realize that Roxana is spying on them.

OLD LADY
Roxana?

PAULA
Yup. The sister-in-law. Javier's sister. She's watching from the window.

The dialogue continues. Paula falls silent. The old man comes over.

> OLD MAN
> You like soap operas, Miss?

> PAULA
> Well, yeah. They're like life, right?

The old man doesn't answer. Paula suddenly realizes this probably isn't the case in his household and tries to make up for it.

> PAULA
> Well, they're fun to watch, aren't they?

EXT. DESERT – NIGHT

The SUV is still in the field, its door open. The light is on inside the car. Salvador and Fernando are moving things around so they can sleep there. Paula appears in the darkness.

> PAULA
> What's taking so long?

> FERNANDO
> We can't change the tire. The jack keeps
> getting stuck.

Paula looks around.

> PAULA
> So we have to sleep here?

> FERNANDO
> (*without stopping what he's doing*)
> Nothing else to do. The nearest town's
> sixty miles from here.

Paula looks around again.

> PAULA
> Hey, you got a flashlight?

> FERNANDO
> What for?

> PAULA
> What do you think?

Fernando hands her a flashlight. She switches it on and heads off down a path.

> FERNANDO
> (*sarcastically, to Salvador*)
> She might walk all the way to Saltillo to find a bathroom.

EXT. DESERT – NIGHT

Paula continues down the path to a grassy spot. Stopping, she points the flashlight to check her surroundings before unbuckling her pants. She crouches down but hears a noise. Flashing the light, she spots a coyote. Looking terrified, she pulls up her pants and runs back to the SUV.

> SALVADOR
> That was fast. Or did something happen?

> PAULA
> (*calmly, hiding her fear*)
> Nope.

INT. SUV – NIGHT

The three of them are lying in the Suburban, its seats pushed back so they can stretch out. Salvador and Fernando are in the back seat and Paula is in the front. Coyotes are howling in the night. Paula wakes up and listens, her eyes wide open.

The howling seems to be getting closer. Paula sits up and looks around the car. She turns on the car lights but sees nothing. She turns off the lights and goes to sleep.

EXT. DESERT – MORNING

Salvador and Paula are rearranging things in the car. Fernando calls them over.

> FERNANDO
> Hey… Come over here…

Paula and Salvador approach. With the toe of his shoe, he points to the spot where the dog's carcass had been. Only bones remain.

> PAULA
> What happened?

> FERNANDO
> (*pointing to footprints on the ground*)
> The coyotes had a feast.

The three look down at the ground. Fernando and Salvador walk away. Paula crouches down and pokes at the bones. She picks up the skull and studies the teeth. Then she looks up toward the bushes in the distance. Standing, she heads over to the Suburban.

> SALVADOR
> Goddamn coyotes, huh?

> PAULA
> Dog-eating coyotes.

They both laugh.

SALVADOR
I know how we could hunt them. Come see...

He leads her around the SUV, opens a suitcase and pulls out a whistle.

SALVADOR
Check this out.

PAULA
What is it?

SALVADOR
A coyote whistle. Check it out.

Salvador blows into it. The whistle makes a high-pitched sound.

SALVADOR
It imitates the sound of an injured hare... So the coyote comes over to eat it and boom! You shoot it.

PAULA
(*looking at the whistle*)
Where did you get that?

SALVADOR
My dad gave it to me.

Paula pauses a moment to think.

PAULA
Fernando told me he died in an accident.

SALVADOR
(*after a beat*)
Yeah, we ran head on into a truck.

                    PAULA
                (*surprised*)
            You were with him.

Salvador nods, slowly. Paula isn't sure what to say.

                    PAULA
            That must have been horrible.

                    SALVADOR
            I don't know. I don't remember a thing.

Fernando, who has been screwing in the tire, straightens up and looks at them both.

EXT. DESERT – MORNING

The old man and the boy bid them farewell. The SUV pulls back onto the road.

INT. SUV – MORNING

Fernando is driving, Salvador in the passenger seat next to him. Paula, in the back seat, looks out the window. She is holding Cecilia, rubbing her head. A gas station appears ahead and Fernando pulls off. It's the same station where his father stopped.

                    ATTENDANT
            How much, kid?

                    FERNANDO
                (*checking his wallet*)
            Give me a hundred... please.

The attendant begins filling the tank. Salvador is looking around, nervous, uncomfortable. Fernando glances at him.

                    FERNANDO
            Is this where you stopped?

SALVADOR
(*doubtful*)
I don't know... No, I don't think so.

FERNANDO
Yes or no?

SALVADOR
I don't know... I'm not sure...

FERNANDO
You gotta remember, dammit!

PAULA
What's going on?

FERNANDO
This idiot doesn't remember where he stopped with Dad.

PAULA
Why do you care?

Fernando glares at her without answering. The attendant comes back and returns the keys to Fernando.

ATTENDANT
You're good, boss.

INT. SUV – NOON

The Suburban continues down the highway, an endless straight line. Salvador is looking more and more nervous. They pass a roadside restaurant and Salvador recognizes it.

SALVADOR
Pull over, pull over...

Fernando turns to his brother.

FERNANDO
Is this where you stopped?

Salvador nods and gazes out toward the highway.

INT. ROADSIDE RESTAURANT – NOON

They go inside. The place is the same as it was when Salvador stopped there with his dad, the same bad taxidermy of a deer's head on the wall. Salvador plops down into a chair. Fernando and Paula look at him, without saying a word. Salvador looks around, taking it all in.

SALVADOR
This is where we ate that afternoon.
(*repeating in a robotic tone*)
This is where…

Fernando sits down next to him.

FERNANDO
You sure?

SALVADOR
Yeah, I'm sure.

Salvador stands up suddenly.

SALVADOR
I'll be right back.

PAULA
Where do you think you're going?

Without answering, Salvador heads toward the bathroom.

INT. BATHROOM – DAY

Salvador enters the bathroom. It looks about the same. He leans against the wall and slaps his forehead with his hand.

INT. ROADSIDE RESTAURANT – DAY

Fernando and Paula are sitting at the table, a couple of sodas on the table in front of them.

>   FERNANDO
>   It was supposed to be my turn.
>
>   PAULA
>   What?
>
>   FERNANDO
>   That trip. I was supposed to go with Dad,
>   not Salvador. But I failed math, so Dad
>   didn't take me.
>
>   PAULA
>   Where were they going?
>
>   FERNANDO
>   Deer hunting in Zaragoza, Coahuila…

Fernando pauses a moment before continuing.

>   FERNANDO
>   I remember the last day I saw him. He
>   was wearing a red shirt and jeans… He
>   told me that if I promised to get an A in
>   math and physics, he'd take me anyway.

He sips his soda before going on.

FERNANDO
I went to pack a bag and I passed my mom in the hall. She asked me what I was doing and when I told her, she got mad. She went to my dad and told her that I was grounded and I wasn't going anywhere. My dad tried to get her to change her mind but it was impossible. They left at around eleven... And... And...

Fernando trails off. Salvador comes in and they sit at the table. They don't speak. A young woman comes over.

WAITRESS
Ready to order?

FERNANDO
(*to Salvador*)
You want something?

Salvador shakes his head. Fernando lifts his chin at Paula as if to ask, "What about you?" but she shakes her head as well.

FERNANDO
How much for the two sodas?

WAITRESS
Five pesos.

Fernando pulls out a coin and leaves it on the table. No one speaks.

INT. SUV – AFTERNOON

The three are silent on the drive. Paula is in the front seat for the first time, holding the squirrel. Salvador looks out at the landscape, his head resting against the window.

PAULA
What did we come here for?

FERNANDO
I already told you.

PAULA
But that's it?

FERNANDO
Yeah, that's it.

Salvador straightens up in his seat.

SALVADOR
That's not true.

Paula turns to him. Fernando glares at him from the rearview mirror.

SALVADOR
We came to find the truck driver who killed my dad.

PAULA
What?

FERNANDO
Don't pay attention to him.

SALVADOR
And you might as well hear this now: we want to find him and kill him.

Paula is dumbstruck.

PAULA
You're messing with me, right?

Neither answers. Paula turns to Fernando.

> PAULA
> That's what you came here for?

Fernando doesn't answer.

> PAULA
> Why didn't you tell me?

Fernando still doesn't answer. Paula raises her voice.

> PAULA
> Listen up, dude. Why didn't you tell me?

Fernando turns and glares at her.

> FERNANDO
> Because this has nothing to do with you, sweetie. Because you can't understand this. Because you just came along to make out with your boyfriend. That's why!

> PAULA
> (*furious*)
> You should have told me... You can't just take me along without mentioning this!

Fernando slams on the brakes and pulls over.

> FERNANDO
> So now you know. OK? What're you going to do? You sticking with us or you bailing?

Paula turns to Salvador.

> PAULA
> This is a lie, right?

She turns back to Fernando, who leans in toward her.

> FERNANDO
> I'm going to kill him. Salvador isn't going to be involved.

Paula looks at Fernando, shaking her head.

> PAULA
> You can't do this. You can't.

> FERNANDO
> No one is asking for your opinion.

Fernando takes off his seatbelt and reaches out his hand to open Paula's door.

> FERNANDO
> So it's settled then. Get out...

Paula's eyes narrow. There's a whole new look on her face, a strange look.

> PAULA
> I already told you: I'll get out when I feel like getting out.

> SALVADOR
> Paula, you gotta understand that...

Paula turns her gaze on him.

> PAULA
> I understand. And I decide when to walk.

> FERNANDO
> Have it your own way! But I'm not responsible for what happens to you.

INT. SUV – AFTERNOON

The Suburban drives down the highway. The three are silent on the drive. Paula's head is resting on the window. She caresses Cecilia's head. They are passing through a wooded spot with a small stream running through it. The road twists and turns.

> PAULA
> Pull over a sec.

> FERNANDO
> What for?

> PAULA
> I gotta pee…

> FERNANDO
> Hold on. It's not far to Nueva Rosita.

> PAULA
> I need to go now. I'll go by the river.
> (*after a beat*)
> Please.

Fernando pulls off to the side of the road. Paula turns the key and pulls it from the ignition. She gets out, closes her door, and turns on the car alarm. The Suburban beeps. She peeps into the window.

> PAULA
> I won't be long.

She heads toward the stream. Fernando and Salvador are silent for a moment.

> FERNANDO
> What the fuck did you tell her for?

SALVADOR
What were you planning on doing?
Bringing her here without saying
anything?

FERNANDO
No. I was planning on getting rid of her
when I had the chance.

Salvador climbs out of the window.

FERNANDO
Where you going, asshole?

Salvador, now out of the car, doesn't answer. He walks toward Paula, who is splashing water on her face. Paula turns to him.

PAULA
I told you I wouldn't be long.

Salvador, looking woeful, stops. Paula straightens up and looks up at the sky.

SALVADOR
What are you going to do?

Paula doesn't answer. She looks at the sun and closes her eyes. Suddenly she turns and goes back to the vehicle.

PAULA
Let's go.

They get to the SUV. Paula turns off the alarm and gets in. Salvador gets in the back seat. Paula takes Cecilia.

PAULA
Ready. Let's go.

EXT. HIGHWAY – DUSK

The SUV leaves the wooded area and is in the desert again.

INT. SUV – AFTERNOON

They are driving more slowly now. Fernando and Salvador are looking out at the landscape. Up ahead off on one side is a small cross.

>   FERNANDO
>   That must be the spot.

Salvador leans out the window.

>   SALVADOR
>   Yup. That's it.

Fernando brings the SUV to a stop.

EXT. PLACE OF THE ACCIDENT – DUSK

The three get out of the Suburban. The cross says "Fernando Villa – RIP." Fernando walks to the middle of the road and looks in both directions. Salvador sits down by the cross without speaking. Tears roll down Fernando's cheeks.

Paula, leaning up against the SUV, is moved. Fernando walks off the road and gathers some stones. He forms a little pile behind the cross and then heads back to find more stones. Without saying a word, Paula and Salvador do the same. At one point, as Paula is looking for stones, she hears a noise, looks up, and comes face to face with a coyote. Their eyes meet for a moment before the coyote turns and disappears.

They form a large pile of rocks behind the cross. When they are finished, Paula pulls out the switchblade she picked up at the hotel, cutting some green branches from a sweet acacia plant and weaving them together. She places the improvised wreath on the little funeral monument. Fernando takes a handful of earth and tosses it to the wind. Paula walks to him and puts her hand on his arm. He turns to her and they gaze at each other without speaking. His face grief-stricken, Fernando wants to say something but can't.

Paula turns, heads to the SUV and takes out Cecilia. She removes the rope from the squirrel's neck and lets her go. The squirrel hides beneath the rocks they have gathered.

INT. SUV – NIGHT

Fernando and Salvador are sleeping in the back of the Suburban, Paula is lying in the front seat, her eyes wide open. From afar, coyotes howl. Paula turns looks back at the sleeping brothers then turns on the radio. Fiddling with the dial, she finds the hit song from the previous day. She listens for a few minutes and then changes the channel until she finds the Monterrey Rancherita and listens to the folk music. When she hears a nearby howl, she lowers the radio volume. She turns on the truck's headlights, watching as the desert landscape is distorted by the beams. Moths flutter around the light. A roadrunner swiftly crosses the halo. Fascinated, Paula gazes out at the window. Then she switches off the lights, turns around, and taps Fernando gently on the shoulder.

                    PAULA
                  (*whispering*)
          Fernando, Fernando…

                  FERNANDO
                  (*waking up*)
   What is it?

Paula pauses a moment before answering.

                  PAULA
   I'm in this with you.

                FERNANDO
        What are you talking about?

                PAULA
        I'm not going to bail. I'll stick with this
        until the end, no matter what happens.

                FERNANDO
        You don't know what you're saying.

                PAULA
        I do know and I won't bail… Good night.

Paula lies down and turns off the radio. But Fernando isn't done talking.

                FERNANDO
    Paula…

                PAULA
        Shhh. You'll wake up Salvador.

EXT. DESERT – DAWN

Paula is sitting on a rock, weaving palm leaves together. Next to her is a half-empty bottle of soda and an open package of Bimbo-brand fruit bread. Fernando, still half asleep, opens the door and gazes at her. He gets out of the car and comes over.

                FERNANDO
    What's up.

                PAULA
        What's up with you.

                FERNANDO
        You been up a while?

PAULA
Half an hour or so.

Paula offers him the fruit bread.

PAULA
Want some?

Fernando sits down next to her and takes a slice. The place looks very different in the sun. White-winged doves can be heard singing.

FERNANDO
About what you said last night: did I dream that or was it true?

PAULA
(*sitting up*)
You dreamed it.

She shows him what she's working on.

PAULA
Look: I made a belt!

FERNANDO
Why are you doing this?

PAULA
I like belts.

FERNANDO
Don't play dumb. You know what I mean.

PAULA
Things always turn out different than you originally thought. Right?

> FERNANDO
> This is serious. We aren't playing around.

> PAULA
> Neither am I.

A coyote appears about sixty yards off. They watch it wander among the thorn trees before it disappears.

INT. SUV – MORNING

They make their way down the highway. Once again, Paula is in the front seat. Everyone looks more relaxed.

> FERNANDO
> Hey, you got any more money?

> PAULA
> Why? You thinking about hitting another dog?

All three laugh.

> PAULA
> I gave you all I had.

Fernando looks as if he doesn't believe her. Paula sticks her hand in her pants pocket and pulls out a few bills.

> PAULA
> This is all I've got.

> FERNANDO
> Come on. Hand it over. All of it.

Paula pulls out one last bill and passes it over. Then she shakes her hands as if to say, "that's all there is."

INT./EXT. HIGHWAY – MORNING

On the highway up ahead, police are doing a stop and search. Without saying a word, Paula takes the gun out from under the seat and tucks it into her pants. She slides the bullets into her pocket. An officer comes over. Fernando rolls down his window.

>   OFFICER
> Good morning.

>   FERNANDO
> Morning, officer.

>   OFFICER
> Where you headed?

>   FERNANDO
>   *(firmly)*
> Piedras Negras.

The officer is studying the interior of the car.

>   OFFICER
> What will you be doing there?

>   PAULA
> Visiting my aunt Maria.

The official steps back and waves them on.

>   OFFICER
> Have a nice trip.

The car advances, and after a beat all three start laughing.

EXT. HIGHWAY/EXIT FOR PIEDRAS NEGRAS – DAY

The SUV takes the exit for Piedras Negras. Fernando pulls into the parking lot of another shabby motel.

> PAULA
> Another of these motels?

> FERNANDO
> (*annoyed*)
> What were you expecting, princess?

> PAULA
> A place where I can get a good night's sleep, a nice shower and a nice meal.

> FERNANDO
> We can't afford any better.

Paula sticks her hand in the back pocket of her pants and pulls out three hundred pesos.

> PAULA
> I'll treat.

> SALVADOR
> (smiling)
> Son of a bitch.

> PAULA
> Nope. "Bitch" will do just fine.

EXT. THREE-STAR HOTEL – DAY

They park out front of a decent-looking hotel and head inside.

Fernando approaches the receptionist.

                    FERNANDO
            Can we get two rooms?

The receptionist takes out some forms. Paula pipes up.

                    PAULA
            He means one room.

Fernando and Salvador, surprised, turn to look at her. Paula repeats herself.

                    PAULA
            We'll take one room, Miss.

The receptionist puts away one of the forms and leaves the other on the counter.

                    RECEPTIONIST
            You paying up front or at checkout?

                    PAULA
            How much is it?

                    RECEPTIONIST
            One hundred.

Paula places a bill on the counter and hands the other two hundreds to Fernando.

                    PAULA
            Now I'm out of money for real.

INT. HOTEL ROOM – DAY

Salvador is lying on one of the beds, Paula on the other. Though it's no five-star hotel, the room has the basics: air conditioning, television, a phone. The shower can be heard in the background.

SALVADOR
Do you miss Eduardo?

PAULA
(*playfully*)
Eduardo... Eduardo who?

SALVADOR
For real. Do you miss him?

PAULA
I don't know. Sometimes I do, sometimes I don't... But I'm leaning more toward "don't."

Fernando emerges from the bathroom wearing clean clothes, his hair wet. He wrinkles up his nose.

FERNANDO
It smells like B.O. in here.

PAULA
Oh, so you're Mr. Clean now, huh?

She enters the bathroom and closes the door. Fernando sits down next to Salvador.

FERNANDO
What do you think? Should we run out on her?

SALVADOR
Why would we?

FERNANDO
This isn't her problem. I don't want her to get into trouble.

SALVADOR
But she told you, she's in this with us…

FERNANDO
Yeah, but she could get nervous and mess things up.

SALVADOR
Don't you trust her?

FERNANDO
I don't know…

SALVADOR
Well, if she's not going, I'm not either.

FERNANDO
Oh, stop it.

SALVADOR
I mean it.

FERNANDO
OK, OK…

He stands up, walks to the door and opens it. He doesn't look too sure of himself.

FERNANDO
I'm going to get something to eat.

He exits. Salvador stays on the bed a moment more and then hurries to the bathroom door to spy on Paula through the keyhole. Naked, she's drying off with the towel.

INT. SUV – AFTERNOON

The SUV is driving at a sluggish pace around town as the three look for street signs.

FERNANDO
What does that one say?

SALVADOR
Juarez.

PAULA
What street you looking for?

FERNANDO
Padre de las Casas Norte.

They continue looking. Suddenly Paula brightens up.

PAULA
That's it. Turn left.

Fernando turns the wheel. They drive two blocks and stop in front of a modest home with peeling paint, number 213. Fernando slows down.

FERNANDO
That's where he lives.

Paula and Salvador turn around. Tense, Fernando speeds up, grasping the wheel forcefully.

INT. RESTAURANT – NIGHT

Salvador and Fernando are eating at a local restaurant. There is a third plate with eggs mixed with beef jerky and a Topo Chico–brand seltzer. The brothers eat without speaking. Paula approaches and sits down.

SALVADOR
What is it?

PAULA
No one answers.

                FERNANDO
        Did you dial it right?

                PAULA
        Yup. 2–24–49. I even memorized it.

                FERNANDO
                (*annoyed*)
        You wouldn't be lying to us now, would
        you?

                PAULA
                (*pissed*)
        If you don't believe me, go call yourself.

Paula pushes a peso coin over to him. Fernando pushes it back, looking down at his plate.

                SALVADOR
        Maybe he changed his number?

Fernando looks up and sighs.

INT. HOTEL ROOM – NIGHT

Fernando and Salvador are sleeping in one bed, Paula in the other. Fernando sits on the edge of the mattress, turns on the bedside light and lifts the phone. He dials a number and lets it ring several times but no one answers. He hangs up, disappointed, and turns to gaze at Paula's back and neck. He reaches out and caresses her. She turns in her sleep but doesn't wake. He turns off the light and goes back to bed.

EXT. STREET – MORNING

Salvador and Fernando are in the SUV, parked a block away from the house. They wait. Paula arrives and gets in.

                    PAULA
Nope. No answer.

                  SALVADOR
Could he have moved?

                  FERNANDO
To Eagle Pass? Who knows.

                    PAULA
I don't think he's far.

                  SALVADOR
                   (*puzzled*)
Why's that?

                    PAULA
When I walked past his house, I saw that
one of the windows was open.

                  FERNANDO
Do you think we could climb on in?

EXT. STREET – DAY

Fernando and Paula are positioned at either end of Estrada's property, keeping an eye on the street. Salvador is walking along a railing on the top floor, his arms out to keep his balance. He reaches the window, pushes it open further, and climbs in. He sees Fernando, who nods in the direction of the front door, which opens a few moments later. Fernando and Paula head in. Fernando pulls out the pistol and leads the way. They walk through the living room. The furniture in the house is modest. They head into the kitchen and are frightened by a cat. Sighing with relief, they continue exploring, heading up the stairs and into the bedrooms. Paula enters the master bedroom.

In the mirror frame, she sees pictures of Estrada with a woman, another with some kids, on a beach, next to his truck, wearing a suit. There is also a woman's portrait that is signed: "To Lucio, with love, Irma." The portrait is hanging across from four sticks of incense, none of them lit. Photographs also line the mirror: there are postcards, matchbox covers, and wedding invitations. Paula is just about to turn away when she notices a newspaper clipping. Moving in closer, she reads the headline: "Tragic Car Accident in Piedras Negras Leaves One Dead." There is a man pictured in a photograph with the caption: "Architect Fernando Villa from Mexico City died in the crash. His young son miraculously survived." Paula calls them in.

PAULA

Hey you guys!

When they come in, Paula shows them the clipping. Fernando's eyes narrow and his nostrils flare. Like Salvador, he looks at it a moment before turning away. Paula pulls off the newspaper clipping, folds it carefully and tucks it away.

EXT. ESTRADA'S HOUSE – DAY

Paula leaves first and looks in both directions before gesturing to them that the coast is clear. Quickly, the three of them get into the SUV. Fernando is clearly worked up by what they have seen. Salvador is mute.

INT. HOTEL ROOM/SUV – NIGHT/DAY

In a series of intercuts, we see them trying the phone number without any luck and watching the house from the SUV.

EXT. THREE–STAR HOTEL – DAY

They leave the three-star hotel and we see them head into the reception of a love motel.

INT. LOVE MOTEL ROOM – DAY

The room is modest. It has an old television, a phone, two queen-sized beds and a dresser. Paula is alone, lying on the bed. "On the Edge of Love" is on, but Paula, looking bored, turns it off. She looks out the window at the city lights, sits down by the dresser, and dials a number. It rings four times and just as she is about to hand up, a voice answers.

                    VOICE
    Hello?

Gasping, Paula hangs up. She takes a deep breath and dials again. The same voice answers: the husky baritone of a 60–year–old man.

                    VOICE
    Yeah, hello? Who's this? Hello?

Without saying a word, Paula hangs up slowly.

EXT. ESTRADA'S HOUSE – DAY

Fernando, leaning against a telephone pole, has his eyes on the front door. The Suburban is parked farther down the street. Salvador and Paula are both in the car. Suddenly, the door to the house opens and a tall, robust man with white hair appears. Closing the door, he starts to walk. Fernando watches him like a hawk. The man walks down the street, Fernando keeping pace with him from the sidewalk on the other side. Fernando looks tense. Estrada walks past the SUV.

INT. SUV – DAY

Paula is in the driver's seat and Salvador, in the passenger seat. Salvador, who is looking back over his shoulder, recognizes the man.

                    SALVADOR
                That's him! That's him.

Paula, trying to be discreet, also turns to look at him. The man walks past the SUV and continues on his way.

                    PAULA
                Are you sure?

                    SALVADOR
                Sure as hell.

Fernando's face appears in the window. His jaw trembles slightly.

                    FERNANDO
                (*breathlessly, to Salvador*)
                Give me the gun.

                    SALVADOR
                (*stunned*)
                Are you gonna kill him?

                    FERNANDO
                Just give it to me!

                    PAULA
                Hold on. Don't do anything crazy.

Salvador looks under the seat but doesn't see the gun. Fernando, exasperated, opens the door and starts searching. Estrada is now a ways down the street. Fernando pulls out the gun. Paula grabs onto his wrist.

                    PAULA
                Don't do anything crazy, goddamn it!

Fernando tries to pull away but Paula won't let go. Salvador, who is in between the two, is not sure what to do. Fernando manages to pull free and when he turns his attention to Estrada, he sees him talking with some women before entering another house.

> FERNANDO
> (*glaring at Paula*)
> Bitch!

INT. RESTAURANT – NIGHT

The three are sitting at a table, all looking worn out. There are few diners this evening. Fernando has a lost look in his eyes.

> FERNANDO
> (*talking almost to himself*)
> We were this close to him…

> PAULA
> There were so many people. We would have gotten caught for sure.

Fernando focuses his anger on her.

> FERNANDO
> Whose side are you on, anyway?

> PAULA
> (*shaking her head*)
> Damn, you really are stupid.

Salvador, who doesn't appear to be listening, turns toward his brother.

> SALVADOR
> (*quiet but firm*)
> Paula's right.

> FERNANDO
> What?

> SALVADOR
> You can't just gun him down in the street.

> FERNANDO
> (*sarcastically*)
> So what... I do a house call?

> SALVADOR
> No. We need to take him someone far from here. Someplace with no one around.

Fernando is about to respond but Salvador continues.

> SALVADOR
> Far from here, Fernando. Got it?

Fernando nods while looking down at the index finger on his right hand.

> FERNANDO
> Yeah. I got it. The problem is going to be keeping this finger from pulling the trigger.

BEGIN MONTAGE:
The three spy on Estrada at different locations across the city. In all of these situations, he appears a quiet, solitary and pleasant man:
–sitting on a park bench.
–grocery shopping.
–out with some little kids.
–talking with friends.

END MONTAGE

EXT. STREET – MORNING

Fernando is leaning against the wall of Estrada's house. The SUV is parked close by, Paula at the wheel and Salvador in the passenger seat. Fernando is holding a sweater. Estrada comes out and Fernando approaches him. Something about the look on Fernando's face surprises Estrada.

                  ESTRADA
Good morning.

Fernando stops a few feet away, visibly nervous.

                  FERNANDO
Well, good morning to you.

He slides the sweater back to reveal the gun.

                  FERNANDO
Get into the car.

Estrada glances over at the SUV and then turns back to Fernando.

                  ESTRADA
What's this about?

                  FERNANDO
Just get in.

                  ESTRADA
I got no money on me, son.

Fernando lets the sweater drop and lifts the gun to the man's face. Without uttering a word, Estrada approaches the vehicle and gets in. Fernando has the gun on him.

FERNANDO
(*to Paula*)
Let's go.

Paula hits the gas and the car jerks forward. After about a half a block, she slams on the breaks.

SALVADOR
What the...

PAULA
The sweater!

Paula jumps out and runs down the block, grabs the sweater, and runs back to the SUV, and speeds off again.

FERNANDO
Are you nuts?

PAULA
What were you thinking? This guy
disappears and when they come looking
for him, there's my sweater!

The SUV speeds down the quiet streets of Piedras Negras. The stoplight turns red and a car stops in front of them. Paula almost rear-ends the other car.

ESTRADA
What's going on? Where are you taking
me?

FERNANDO
(*pointing the gun in his face*)
Shut up, prick.

Paula starts speeding as soon as the light turns green. At the next intersection, she looks suddenly confused.

FERNANDO
(*to Estrada*)
Which way out of town?

ESTRADA
(*in a menacing tone*)
Right.

FERNANDO
You better not be lying.

Paula turns right, goes a few blocks and stops.

PAULA
What now?

ESTRADA
Left. Then right at the next corner.

FERNANDO
You better not be fucking with us.

They end up on a wide road. Paula joins the other cars, which are speeding along. This dead-ends at a narrow freeway. Paula follows it. A few miles on, they come to a dirt road.

FERNANDO
Pull over a sec.

Paula stops.

FERNANDO
(*to Estrada*)
Where does that lead?

ESTRADA
It goes along the Rio Bravo.

Fernando gestures for Paula to head in that direction. The SUV makes its way down the dirt road, dust rising in its wake. In the distance, they can see the river. The truck drives a while before stopping before a grove of thorny trees.

> FERNANDO
> (to Estrada)
> Get out. Don't try anything funny or I'll
> blow your head off.

Estrada gets out and Fernando follows him, the gun on him at all times.

EXT. DESERT – DAY

Estrada and Fernando are standing by the SUV. Salvador approaches with a rope.

> FERNANDO
> (to Salvador)
> Tie him to that tree.

They walk over to the tree.

> SALVADOR
> Hands behind your back.

Estrada, unafraid, meets his eyes. Fernando has the gun on him. Estrada sits down, his back against the trunk, and stretches his hands out behind him. Salvador ties him up tightly.

> ESTRADA
> That's too tight.

> SALVADOR
> Shut up.

Paula brings another rope and Salvador ties Estrada around the waist. Estrada looks up at Fernando.

ESTRADA
You wanna tell me what this is about?

Fernando ignores him and looks away. Estrada kicks the ground, covering Fernando's pants with dust, but Fernando doesn't react. Estrada then turns to Paula.

ESTRADA
What are you all after? Money? I ain't got any.

FERNANDO
Do we look like we need money?

Estrada is taken aback by the question.

FERNANDO
Is that what we look like to you? Thieves? Huh? Is that what we look like?

ESTRADA
(*in a pleading tone*)
So what is it? What are you all after?

Paula approaches, pulls out the newspaper clipping, unfolds it, and places it on Estrada's lap. Estrada shakes his head.

ESTRADA
I don't believe this.

FERNANDO
Don't believe what, you son of a bitch?

ESTRADA
It was an accident.

Fernando takes the photograph of his father and holds it in front of Estrada's face.

                    FERNANDO
            You killed him!

                    ESTRADA
            That's not what happened...

                    SALVADOR
                    (*exasperated*)
            It was your fault!

                    ESTRADA
            It wasn't anyone's fault: it was just an
            accident. Simple as that.

Fernando takes a few steps back, takes the safety off the gun and points it at him.

                    FERNANDO
            Simple as this...

Estrada's breath becomes shallow and raspy. He is terrified and sweating, but he continues to meet Fernando's gaze.

                    SALVADOR
            It was your fault!

Paula looks on, eyes wide. Fernando takes a step forward. He seems to have made up his mind.

                    FERNANDO
            You killed him.

Estrada looks down toward the ground, as if waiting for the bullet.

                    ESTRADA
            No, no, no...

Estrada takes shaky, shallow breaths. He looks back up at Fernando, who points the gun at him a few seconds more but then lowers it.

> FERNANDO
> Fucking shitbag.

He tucks the weapon into his belt and walks away. Paula and Salvador follow him. Estrada inhales audibly.

EXT. DESERT – DAY

The rushing water of the Rio Bravo can be heard from afar. The truck is parked beneath a tall mesquite. Paula, Salvador and Fernando are off to one side, sitting around a fire, where eggs are cooking in a frying pan. Once in a while, Salvador pokes at them with a spoon. About ten yards away is Estrada, his back to them. Salvador takes the eggs off the fire, divides them among three dishes, and hands one each to Paula and Fernando.

> PAULA
> Hey, we gonna feed him?

> FERNANDO
> No.

Salvador takes the gun, which is lying on a rock, tucks it into his belt and takes his dish over to Estrada. He sits on a rock and starts to eat. Seeing him approach, Estrada tries to start up a conversation.

> ESTRADA
> Pretty hot out, huh?

Salvador doesn't speak, just nods his head.

ESTRADA
(*licking his lips*)
Could you get me some water? Please.

Salvador puts his plate down and walks over to the others. He takes a cup and pours some water.

FERNANDO
(*to Salvador*)
What are you doing?

SALVADOR
Giving him water.

FERNANDO
No.

SALVADOR
You want him to die of thirst?

FERNANDO
I don't give a fuck how he dies.

Ignoring his brother, Salvador takes the water to Estrada and lifts the cup to his lips. The Estrada gulps down the water so desperately that a good part of it spills on his clothes.

ESTRADA
(*finishing*)
Could you get me some more?

SALVADOR
No.

Salvador sits back down on the rock, picks up his dish, and continues eating.

EXT. DESERT – AFTERNOON

It's about 3pm. The heat is now so extreme that the horizon looks blurry. Paula and Salvador are sitting in the truck listening to the radio. The gun is on the rock. Estrada is sweating so bad his shirt is sopping. He shakes his head from time to time, trying to shoo away the flies and mosquitos.

INT. SUV – AFTERNOON

> PAULA
> I like it more and more.

> SALVADOR
> What?

Paula points to the radio.

> PAULA
> The Monterrey Rancherita!

Salvador smiles.

> PAULA
> What's your favorite music?

> SALVADOR
> (*thinking*)
> Rock. U2, Red Hot Chili Peppers,
> sometimes Metallica and, believe it or not,
> Elvis Presley.

> PAULA
> (*laughing*)
> Elvis? That's for old people!

> SALVADOR
> What about you?

PAULA
I don't even know what I like any more.

They both smile. Something in the underbrush catches Paula's eye.

PAULA
Look.

It's a coyote. Salvador turns off the radio and pulls the whistle out of the glove compartment.

SALVADOR
Let's see if this thing actually works.

Without moving from the passenger seat, Salvador blows the whistle a few seconds, and just when she's just about to stop, Paula points toward the coyote.

PAULA
(*whispering*)
It's coming.

Salvador blows the whistle again. Excited, Paula scans the buses, hoping the predator will show itself. Suddenly it appears, about twelve yards from the truck.

PAULA
Keep going.

Paula gets out of the truck, crouches down and goes for the gun. When she comes back, the coyote is standing there, trying to find where the sound is coming from. Paula lifts the gun, points, and shoots. The coyote takes off running but Paula fires again. The bullet strikes the coyote, who continues running, whimpering with pain.

PAULA
I got him! I got him!

Fernando comes running over.

>   FERNANDO
> What is it?

>   PAULA
>   (*excited*)
> I shot a coyote!

>   SALVADOR
> Yeah! Paula got one!

Furious, Fernando yanks the gun away from her.

>   FERNANDO
> Are you crazy? You want the whole
> world to find out we're here?

The coyote's howls slowly fade as it gets further away. Estrada is tied to the tree, his breathing uneven.

EXT. DESERT – AFTERNOON

Salvador and Paula are cooking over the fire. Sitting on a rock, Fernando is drinking some soda, his eye on Estrada, the gun on his lap. Estrada rolls his neck a few times, as if something were bothering him. He scratches himself against the tree trunk. After several attempts, he tries to turn toward Fernando, who is behind him, outside his line of vision.

>   ESTRADA
> Hey... hey!

Fernando doesn't answer. Estrada tries again.

>   ESTRADA
> Hey... listen!

Fernando stands up and walks over to him.

FERNANDO
What do you want?

ESTRADA
Something is inside my shirt and it's biting me... Can you get it off? Please.

Fernando approaches Estrada and peers down his sweaty neck.

FERNANDO
Where?

ESTRADA
Down below the shoulder.

Fernando lifts the shirt and sees a weevil crawling down Estrada's back. Pulling it off, he tosses it aside. Estrada looks up at him, thankful.

ESTRADA
What's your name?

FERNANDO
What do you care?

ESTRADA
Fernando?

Estrada smiles. Fernando looks surprised.

ESTRADA
That's right, isn't it? Like your dad... You look so much like him.

Fernando's whole expression changes.

FERNANDO
(*furious*)
My dad was more than just a photograph,
you prick. How the hell would you know
I look like him?

Estrada doesn't speak for a moment. He looks down a second and then raises his head to look into Fernando's eyes.

ESTRADA
Because I've dreamed about that picture
every night since.

Now it's Fernando who looks away.

EXT. DESERT – NIGHT

It's a clear night dimly lit by the moon. From afar, coyotes howl. Salvador is asleep in the truck. Paula and Fernando are sitting across from the fire. Estrada, his eyes wide open, tries to listen in on their conversation. Paula reaches into her back and pulls out the rattlesnake. She bites off a piece and starts to chew.

PAULA
You should try this.

FERNANDO
How does it taste?

PAULA
Good... Better with lemon.

Fernando takes the rattlesnake, pulls off a chunk, squeezes a lemon over it, and puts it in his mouth. Chewing slowly, he nods. Paula smiles.

FERNANDO
My dad would give me all sorts of
things to try: iguana, opossum, squirrel,
hare, deer, quail. He said you have to
try everything, smell everything, see
everything...

PAULA
Your dad was pretty cool, huh.

FERNANDO
Yeah, a great guy. The best.

After a beat, Fernando looks up at Paula.

FERNANDO
What about your mom?

PAULA
My mom? I don't know. I never met her.
She died when I was just a baby. All I
know about her are things I've heard. Or
pictures. My dad says I look like her. At
least you knew your dad.

FERNANDO
Maybe it would have been better not
knowing him.

Again, neither speaks. They are alone with their thoughts. Paula looks sad. Fernando lifts her chin and stares into her eyes a moment. They start to kiss and a moment later, they are all over each other. Estrada can hear their heavy breathing. Suddenly, Paula stops and looks into Fernando's eyes.

FERNANDO
What is it?

Paula looks at him a moment more.

> PAULA
> Nothing... nothing...

They continue making out and start pulling each other's clothes off. Paula lies down on the blanket where they were sitting and whispers into Fernando's ear.

> PAULA
> Take it slow... Please... Go slowly.

Estrada, tied to the tree, cannot see Fernando and Paula but he hears them making love.

EXT. DESERT – MORNING

The three are eating fruit bread. Water is boiling over the fire. The sun is just coming up. Paula takes two pieces of the fruit bread and a glass of milk to Estrada. She kneels down.

> PAULA
> Here you are.

> ESTRADA
> Aren't you going to untie me to eat?

> PAULA
> No.

> ESTRADA
> What if I gotta pee?

> PAULA
> When that happens, we'll see.

> ESTRADA
> I need to go since yesterday... I held it in all night.

PAULA

Eat first.

Paula lifts a piece of fruit bread to his mouth and he takes a bite.

ESTRADA
(*in a slightly mocking tone*)
A nice night, wasn't it?

PAULA
(*her eyes narrowing*)
Yeah. A lot of stars.

Estrada takes another bite and swallows before continuing.

ESTRADA
Your boyfriend really loves you.

Paula studies him for a moment.

PAULA
(*after a beat*)
He's not my boyfriend.

ESTRADA
(*confused*)
What?

PAULA
(*firmly*)
He's my brother.

Estrada's eyes widen. Paula lifts another piece of fruit bread to his mouth, then stands up,

PAULA
I'll tell my brother to untie you now so you can pee.

EXT. TREES/DESERT – DAY

Estrada is peeing alongside a tree. He glances over at Fernando, who is three steps away, pointing the gun at his head.

ESTRADA
You gonna let me go again later?

Fernando shrugs. They walk a few steps and Estrada stops. He points to something lying between some prickly cacti. It's the coyote Paula shot, still breathing but unconscious. Fernando keeps the gun on Estrada. The bullet wound is visible on the coyote's back, which is covered with blood and flies.

ESTRADA
Why not finish him off?

FERNANDO
No.

ESTRADA
Well, it won't take long for him to die anyway.

They continue on to their camp. Estrada stops and looks Fernando in the eye.

ESTRADA
What are you going to do with me?

Fernando doesn't answer and gestures with the gun for him to continue walking.

ESTRADA
(*taking a deep breath*)
You look like a good kid from a good family. How about you let me go and we forget this whole thing?

Fernando doesn't answer. After a beat, Fernando's eyes narrow.

> FERNANDO
> Keep walking.

Estrada doesn't move. Fernando lifts the gun and points it straight at his chest. Getting the idea he means business, Estrada walks back to the tree.

EXT. DESERT – MORNING

The three of them are sweating profusely in the morning heat.

> PAULA
> Boy, is it hot. How about we go for a dip in the river?

> SALVADOR
> I like that idea.

> FERNANDO
> You go. I'll stay and look after him.

Paula goes to the truck and pulls out a bathing suit and a pair of shorts.

> PAULA
> I came prepared, guys!

She tosses the shorts to Salvador.

> PAULA
> See if they fit.

EXT. RIVER – DAY

Salvador and Paula are both changing at different spots near the shores of the Rio Bravo.

> SALVADOR
> You think it's deep?

> PAULA
> No idea... You know how to swim?

> SALVADOR
> I mean, sort of.

> PAULA
> You're with a high school champ. I'll keep an eye on you. Come on. We can go shopping across the border!

They swim across the river to the U.S. side.

> PAULA
> Easy crossing the border, huh? You swim a little and you're there.

> SALVADOR
> (*looking inland*)
> Everything changes on this side... It's a different world.

> PAULA
> That's the way life should be. You know exactly where one thing ends and another begins.

Paula stands up and runs back to the river.

> PAULA
> Let's see who makes it back to Mexico first!

They splash in the water, swim back to the Mexican side and rest on the shore. Paula takes a few steps down the shore while Salvador gazes at the river. Suddenly, Paula calls to him.

PAULA
Salvador...

When Salvador turns to look, she takes off her bikini top. Salvador is shocked and turned on.

PAULA
Never spy on me again.

Now she takes off her bikini bottom.

PAULA
From now on, if you want to see me naked, just ask.

Salvador stands up and approaches her, breathing heavily. He looks her up and down. Paula leans in and kisses his cheek.

PAULA
Let's go.

Grabbing her bikini, she heads toward the desert where the rest of her clothes are lying. Visibly shaken, Salvador watches her leave.

EXT. DESERT – AFTERNOON

Paula is sleeping in the front seat of the truck. Fernando is in the back seat. Salvador is keeping an eye on Estrada.

ESTRADA
Can you untie me? I gotta pee.

SALVADOR
You got to wait for my brother to wake up.

ESTRADA
What do I do in the meantime?

SALVADOR
Just hold it in, I guess.

Neither speaks for a moment.

ESTRADA
How about letting me go and we get this over with?

Salvador shakes his head.

ESTRADA
Untie me quick. Your brother won't ever know.

SALVADOR
No.

Estrada studies his face for a moment.

ESTRADA
You were the one in the car with him, is that right?

Salvador nods and gazes out toward the highway.

ESTRADA
Then know it was an accident, that it happened because…

SALVADOR
Yeah, I know. I know it was an accident.

ESTRADA
So you know… You know it wasn't on purpose, right? I fell asleep. I was

exhausted. I had been working three days straight. You got any idea what that's like?

SALVADOR

I can imagine.

ESTRADA

I haven't been OK since... I was sick over what happened...

Salvador's eyes narrow, his face tenses.

SALVADOR

That's a goddamn lie... All you cared about was getting the hell out of there. While we were trapped inside a burning metal box.

ESTRADA

You gotta understand that...

SALVADOR
(*raising his voice*)
My dad covered with blood, dying, and me wanting to get out of the car to help him and you running away, like a goddamn rat instead of coming back to help me get out...

ESTRADA

Just a minute now, I couldn't have...

SALVADOR

I stunk of gasoline and Dad kept trying to say something but he couldn't breathe! He was choking on his own blood and I couldn't reach him!

Salvador's shouting wakes Paula and Fernando. They approach and see he is worked into a fury.

> SALVADOR
> And you ran. And you let him die! And he was covered with blood...

> FERNANDO
> What's going on?

> SALVADOR
> (*crying*)
> This son of a bitch ran. He didn't even try to help. And Dad was gasping for breath, dying...

Salvador trails off. Fernando can't bear to see his brother like this. He takes the gun and points it just inches from Estrada's face.

> FERNANDO
> (*to Estrada*)
> You motherfucker.

Estrada gasps in terror.

> ESTRADA
> No, no...

> FERNANDO
> Fuck it all...

It seems like he's going to shoot. But suddenly, Fernando lowers the gun, his hand trembling, and shakes his head. He takes a step back and slams Estrada in the mouth with the butt of the gun. The blow whips his head to the side, blood steaming from his nose and mouth. Paula watches, shocked and shaken.

FADE OUT

EXT. DESERT – NIGHT

Salvador is lying in the truck. Paula and Fernando make out next to the fire. Neither speaks. They get undressed and start making love. Salvador watches them for a moment from the car window. Then he leans back, pulls up the blanket, and closes his eyes.

EXT. RIVER – MORNING

Salvador and Paula are sitting on the shore of the Rio Bravo. They are fully dressed. The day is cloudy and cold. They watch the flowing currents in silence. Salvador gets up, picks up a handful of pebbles, and throws them into the water. Something seems to be weighing on him.

EXT. CAMP – MORNING

Estrada is still tied up. He looks tired and defeated. Fernando is next to him, drinking coffee, the gun resting on his lap.

ESTRADA
(*in a desperate voice*)
Untie me… I gotta pee.

Fernando ignores him.

ESTRADA
I'm talking to you, kid.

Fernando turns toward him, glaring.

FERNANDO
Pee your pants or rot in hell for all I care.

Estrada glares at him. Fernando meets his eyes for only a moment, then looks away.

EXT. DESERT – DAY

Salvador and Paula return to camp. They make their way through the underbrush and discover the coyote Paula shot. It is dead and swollen, its jaw sagging. A trail of ants leads to and from its eyes. Paula squats down and touches the bullet wound, staining her fingers with blood. Standing up, she glances down at them, unmoved.

> SALVADOR
> He's a male.

Paula looks him and tilts her head.

> SALVADOR
> (*repeating himself*)
> The coyote. He's a male.

Paula looks down at the blood on her fingers and nods, without any sign of emotion.

EXT. CAMP – AFTERNOON

Salvador, Paula and Fernando are eating around the fire. No one speaks. Estrada has his eyes closed, his head lolling forward. He has pissed himself and looks dirty, humiliated, defeated.

FADE OUT

INT. SUV – NIGHT

Coyotes are howling in the night. Salvador and Fernando are sleeping in the back of the Suburban, Paula in the front. Salvador sits up quietly and leans into the front seat. He gazes at Paula for a moment and then begins unbuttoning her blouse. She wakes with a start.

                    SALVADOR
Shhh...

                    PAULA
What are you doing?

                    SALVADOR
Shhh... I want to see you...

                    PAULA
No.

                    SALVADOR
That's what you said.

                    PAULA
Not now...

                    SALVADOR
It's what you said... please.

Paula sighs and unbuttons the rest of the blouse herself. Her breasts are lit by the moon. Salvador, hesitant, lifts his hand and starts caressing her.

EXT. DESERT – MORNING

It is cloudy and cold. Paula rubs her arms to warm up. Fernando is trying to light the fire. Salvador is drinking from a mug. Suddenly, a drop of rain falls. Fernando gazes up at the sky and more drops fall. Paula grabs the equipment that is around the fire and puts everything away. She also takes the newspaper clipping with Fernando Villa's picture and tucks it into a pocket. Estrada looks up at the sky and feels the rain on his face. He struggles to turn and see what his captors are doing. The rain is falling faster.

                    SALVADOR
                (*pointing toward Estrada*)
            What do we do with him?

                    FERNANDO
            I don't know.

It's pouring. Fernando runs to the truck and jumps in next to Paula. Salvador walks toward Estrada but stops halfway there. He takes one more step in that direction but then turns, and runs back to the truck. Estrada tries to yank himself free from the ropes.

INT. SUV – MORNING

The three watch the rain pounding on the windshield.

EXT. DESERT – MORNING

The storm passes and the sky begins to clear. The three get out of the truck and walk to where Estrada is. He is soaking wet, trembling from the cold, and desperate.

                    ESTRADA
            Untie me.

No one speaks.

                    ESTRADA
            Please… I'm so stiff. The rope is digging
            into me. Let me go.

Fernando nods in Salvador's direction and Salvador unties him. Untied, Estrada rubs his wrists. He looks exhausted, defeated, and in pain. With some effort, he stands. He is trembling, drops running down his face. He moves his arms in circles to try to warm up and shakes his head. He takes a few steps and Fernando stops him, raising the gun.

FERNANDO
Where do you think you're going?

Estrada ignores him and continues walking.

FERNANDO
Stop right there.

Fernando lifts the gun and points it straight at his chest. Estrada stops.

ESTRADA
Go ahead, kill me, but don't fuck with me anymore…

Estrada continues on his way. Fernando follows him, the gun still on him. Paula and Salvador are following behind. Estrada walks a bit faster now and leaves Fernando behind. Fernando watches him go and realizes he is no longer afraid. Paula catches up to Fernando, takes the gun and runs up to Estrada, who stops. There is a glimmer in her eye.

PAULA
Don't take one more step.

Estrada shakes his head and continues. Paula points the gun right at his chest.

PAULA
Don't move.

Estrada takes a single step and Paula shoots. Salvador and Fernando both turn toward her, horrified. Estrada stops. She has fired into the air but now she has the gun pointing at his chest.

PAULA
One more step and I'll kill you.

Estrada knows she's not bluffing. Paula turns toward Fernando and Salvador.

> PAULA
> Hey you guys!

The two walk over. Paula turns her attention back to Estrada.

> PAULA
> Get on your knees and tell them you're sorry.

Estrada doesn't look like he plans to obey. Paula shoots the ground, three times, right next to him.

> PAULA
> Do what I say.

Estrada remains standing but begins to sob.

> ESTRADA
> I didn't mean… I didn't mean…

He can't get the words out. Salvador and Fernando are watching him, both looking as if they might cry. Paula's eyes are cold.

> PAULA
> You tell them you're sorry, you motherfucker.

Estrada looks up. He is sobbing so hard he can't speak. Calmly, Salvador approaches Paula and gestures for the gun.

> SALVADOR
> Pass it over.

Paula turns to him. Salvador is crying too.

                    SALVADOR
              Give me the gun.

Paula hands him the weapon. Salvador points it toward Estrada. It seems for a moment like he will shoot but at the last moment, he points toward the sky and fires the last two shots. He looks at Estrada and tosses the gun aside. Salvador's eyes meet Estrada's. Estrada tries to speak but can't. He is shaking and can't stop crying. Paula's eyes fill with tears. Salvador takes a few steps toward Estrada and stops across from him.

                    SALVADOR
              We forgive you.

He then walks past him toward the Suburban. Fernando and Paula glance at each other and then follow him. Before they depart, Estrada and Fernando exchange one final glance.

Paula, Salvador and Fernando gets into the truck. Fernando starts it up and steps on the gas. The truck takes off, skidding through the mud. Estrada watches them go, tears streaming down his face.

EXT. HIGHWAY – AFTERNOON

The clouds have passed, leaving the sky a clear blue. The truck is making its way down the highway.

INT. SUV – DUSK

No one speaks. Fernando pulls over. There are no other cars in sight. Fernando stares straight ahead. Without a word, the three of them contemplate the horizon. A coyote crosses the road and the three of them watch it. It stops for a moment, looks up at them, and disappears into the underbrush.

                    PAULA
              Should we head home?

Fernando turns toward her. He looks at her for a moment and nods.

                    FERNANDO
     Yeah.

He shifts gears and drives back onto the asphalt. The sun begins to break through the clouds.

EXT. HIGHWAY/DESERT – AFTERNOON

The Suburban makes its way in a straight line across the desert.

www.ingramcontent.com/pod-product-compliance
Lightning Source LLC
Chambersburg PA
CBHW070145080526
44586CB00015B/1844